Di Su
Editor

MW01518003

Collection Development Issues in the Online Environment

Collection Development Issues in the Online Environment has been co-published simultaneously as *The Acquisitions Librarian*, Volume 19, Numbers 1/2 (#37/38) 2007.

Pre-publication REVIEWS, COMMENTARIES, EVALUATIONS . . .

More pre-publication
REVIEWS, COMMENTARIES, EVALUATIONS . . .

"**A** USEFUL SUMMARY of the multiplicity of issues plaguing those librarians who attempt to manage electronic resources. Particularly interesting were the chapters on the variability of indexing of the same journals in different databases, the workflow and troubleshooting involved in digitizing a collection of business annual reports, and the futility of trying to unbundle the cost of print vs. electronic journals as a cost-saving measure."

Patricia S. Banach, MLS, MA
Director of Library Services
J. Eugene Smith Library
Eastern Connecticut State University

"**H**ere are some highlights: Crothers, Prabhu, and Sullivan describe the real-life trials and tribulations of providing access to electronic journals in a large academic library. Anyone who has tried to establish access to an electronic journal will enjoy reading this chapter and reliving some of the more frustrating moments in this process. Cronin-Kardon and Halperin describe the creation of a digital collection of annual reports that are now freely available on the World Wide Web. It is useful to understand all the steps needed to successfully digitize potentially fragile material. The real gem of this volume, however, is the overview of copyright issues of electronic resources for those in acquisitions and collection development. Lee and Wu have provided an excellent explanation of the murky waters of copyright in a clear and well-organized manner."

Susan Davis, MLS
Head
Electronic Periodicals Management Department
University at Buffalo (SUNY)

The Haworth Information Press®
An Imprint of The Haworth Press, Inc.

Collection Development Issues in the Online Environment

Collection Development Issues in the Online Environment has been co-published simultaneously as *The Acquisitions Librarian*, Volume 19, Numbers 1/2 (#37/38) 2007.

Monographic Separates from *The Acquisitions Librarian*™

For additional information on these and other Haworth Press titles, including descriptions, tables of contents, reviews, and prices, use the QuickSearch catalog at http://www.HaworthPress.com.

Collection Development Issues in the Online Environment, edited by Di Su (Vol. 19, No. 1/2 #37/38, 2007). *"Encompassing both common and special issues, this book explores the current and future landscapes of collecting in an online environment. THIS INTRIGUING ANALYSIS IS WELL WORTH THE READ for an acquisitions or collection development practitioner who is currently grappling with the challenges of maintaining a pertinent electronic collection."* (Aisha Harvey, MSLS, Collection Development/Reference Librarian, Duke University)

Integrating Print and Digital Resources in Library Collections, edited by Audrey Fenner (No. 35/36, 2006). *Examines the formats and technologies involved in combining print and electronic materials to form a thoroughly integrated library collection.*

Managing Digital Resources in Libraries, edited by Audrey Fenner (No. 33/34, 2005). *A practical guide to managing library materials in digital formats; examines innovations including the integration of PDA-accessible resources into collections and the developmnet of all-digital libraries.*

Selecting Materials for Library Collections, edited by Audrey Fenner (No. 31/32, 2004). *A comprehensive overview of building, maintaining, and updating any library collection.*

Collection Development Policies: New Directions for Changing Collections, edited by Daniel C. Mack (No. 30, 2003). *An in-depth guide to building and maintaining effective policy statements.*

Acquisitions in Different and Special Subject Areas, edited by Abulfazal M. Fazle Kabir (No. 29, 2003). *Presents profiles, methods, and processes for acquisitions in specialized subject areas, including local and regional poetry, oceanography, educational information in electronic formats, popular fiction collections, regional and ethnic materials, and more.*

Strategic Marketing in Library and Information Science, edited by Irene Owens (No. 28, 2002). *"A useful overview of marketing for LIS practitioners in a number of settings, including archives, public libraries, and LIS schools."* (Barbara B. Moran, PhD, Professor, School of Information and Library Science, University of North Carolina-Chapel Hill)

Out-of-Print and Special Collection Materials: Acquisition and Purchasing Options, edited by Judith Overmier (No. 27, 2002). *"Offers inspiration and advice to everyone who works with a special collection. Other librarians and bibliophiles who read it will come away with a new appreciation of the challenges and achievements of special collections librarians. . . . Also valuable for teachers who address these aspects of library work."* (Peter Barker, PhD, Professor of the History of Science, University of Oklahoma, Norman)

Publishing and the Law: Current Legal Issues, edited by A. Bruce Strauch (No. 26, 2001). Publishing and the Law: Current Legal Issues *provides lawyers and librarians with insight into the main areas of legal change that are having an impact on the scholarly publishing world today. This book explores constitutional issues, such as the Communications Decency Act, showing how the First Amendment makes it virtually impossible to regulate the World Wide Web. This unique book includes a history of copyright law up through current international treaties to provide an understanding of how copyright law and the electronic environment intertwine.*

Readers, Reading and Librarians, edited by Bill Katz (No. 25, 2001). *Reaffirms the enthusiasm of books and readers as libraries evolve from reading centers to information centers where librarians are now also web masters, information scientists, and media experts.*

Acquiring Online Management Reports, edited by William E. Jarvis (No. 24, 2000). *This fact-filled guide explores a broad variety of issues involving acquisitions and online management reports to keep libraries and library managers current with changing technology and, ultimately, offer patrons more information. This book provides you with discussions and suggestions on several* topics, including working with vendors, developing cost-effective collection development methods to suit your library, assessing collection growth, and choosing the best electronic resources to help meet your goals. Acquiring Online Management Reports *offers you an array of proven ideas, options, and examples that will enable your library to keep up with client demands and simplify the process of collecting, maintaining, and interpreting online reports.*

The Internet and Acquisitions: Sources and Resources for Development, edited by Mary E. Timmons (No. 23, 2000). *"For those trying to determine how the Internet could be of use to their particular library in the area of acquisitions, or for those who have already decided they should be moving in that direction . . . this volume is a good place to begin." (James Mitchell, MLS, Library Director, Bainbridge-Guilford Central School, Bainbridge, NY)*

Gifts and Exchanges: Problems, Frustrations, . . . and Triumphs, edited by Catherine Denning (No. 22, 1999). *"A complete compendium embracing all aspects of the matter in articles that are uniformly well-written by people experienced in this field." (Jonathan S. Tryon, CAL, JD, Professor, Graduate School of Library and Information Studies, University of Rhode Island)*

Periodical Acquisitions and the Internet, edited by Nancy Slight-Gibney (No. 21, 1999). *Sheds light on the emerging trends in selection, acquisition, and access to electronic journals.*

Public Library Collection Development in the Information Age, edited by Annabel K. Stephens (No. 20, 1998). *"A first-rate collection of articles . . . This is an engaging and helpful work for anyone involved in developing public library collections." (Lyn Hopper, MLn, Director, Chestatee Regional Library, Dahlonega, GA)*

Fiction Acquisition/Fiction Management: Education and Training, edited by Georgine N. Olson (No. 19, 1998). *"It is about time that attention is given to the collection in public libraries . . . it is about time that public librarians be encouraged to treat recreational reading with the same respect that is paid to informational reading . . . Thank you to Georgine Olson for putting this volume together." (Regan Robinson, MLS, Editor and Publisher, Librarian Collection Letter)*

Acquisitions and Collection Development in the Humanities, edited by Irene Owens (No. 17/18, 1997). *"Can easily become a personal reference tool." (William D. Cunningham, PhD, Retired faculty, College of Library and Information Service, University of Maryland, College Park)*

Approval Plans: Issues and Innovations, edited by John H. Sandy (No. 16, 1996). *"This book is valuable for several reasons, the primary one being that librarians in one-person libraries need to know how approval plans work before they can try one for their particular library . . . An important addition to the professional literature." (The One-Person Library)*

Current Legal Issues in Publishing, edited by A. Bruce Strauch (No. 15, 1996). *"Provides valuable access to a great deal of information about the current state of copyright thinking." (Library Association Record)*

New Automation Technology for Acquisitions and Collection Development, edited by Rosann Bazirjian (No. 13/14, 1995). *"Rosann Bazirjian has gathered together 13 current practitioners who explore technology and automation in acquisitions and collection development . . . Contains something for everyone." (Library Acquisitions: Practice and Theory)*

Management and Organization of the Acquisitions Department, edited by Twyla Racz and Rosina Tammany (No. 12, 1994). *"Brings together topics and librarians from across the country to discuss some basic challenges and changes facing our profession today." (Library Acquisitions: Practice and Theory)*

A. V. in Public and School Libraries: Selection and Policy Issues, edited by Margaret J. Hughes and Bill Katz (No. 11, 1994). *"Many points of view are brought forward for those who are creating new policy or procedural documents . . . Provide[s] firsthand experience as well as considerable background knowledge. . . ." (Australian Library Review)*

Published by

The Haworth Information Press®, 10 Alice Street, Binghamton, NY 13904-1580 USA

The Haworth Information Press® is an imprint of The Haworth Press, Inc., 10 Alice Street, Binghamton, NY 13904-1580 USA.

Collection Development Issues in the Online Environment has been co-published simultaneously as *The Acquisitions Librarian*™, Volume 19, Numbers 1/2 (#37/38) 2007.

The development, preparation, and publication of this work has been undertaken with great care. However, the publisher, employees, editors, and agents of The Haworth Press and all imprints of The Haworth Press, Inc., including The Haworth Medical Press® and Pharmaceutical Products Press®, are not responsible for any errors contained herein or for consequences that may ensue from use of materials or information contained in this work. Opinions expressed by the author(s) are not necessarily those of The Haworth Press, Inc. With regard to case studies, identities and circumstances of individuals discussed herein have been changed to protect confidentiality. Any resemblance to actual persons, living or dead, is entirely coincidental.

The Haworth Press is committed to the dissemination of ideas and information according to the highest standards of intellectual freedom and the free exchange of ideas. Statements made and opinions expressed in this publication do not necessarily reflect the views of the Publisher, Directors, management, or staff of The Haworth Press, Inc., or an endorsement by them.

Cover design by Karen M. Lowe.

Library of Congress Cataloging-in-Publication Data

Collection development issues in the online environment / Di Su, editor.
     p. cm.
    "Co-published simultaneously as The acquisitions librarian, volume 19, numbers 1/2 2007."
    Includes bibliographical references and index.
    ISBN-13: 978-0-7890-3086-3 (alk. paper)
    ISBN-10: 0-7890-3086-1 (alk. paper)
    ISBN-13: 978-0-7890-3087-0 (pbk. : alk. paper)
    ISBN-10: 0-7890-3087-X (pbk. : alk. paper)
    1. Academic libraries–Collection development. 2. Libraries–Special collections–Electronic information resources. 3. Libraries–Special collections–Electronic journals. 4. Acquisition of electronic information resources. 5. Acquisition of electronic journals. 6. Libraries and electronic publishing. 7. Digital libraries–Collection development. I. Su, Di.

Z687.C642 2007
025.2'832–dc22

2005018383

Collection Development Issues in the Online Environment

Di Su
Editor

Collection Development Issues in the Online Environment has been co-published simultaneously as *The Acquisitions Librarian*, Volume 19, Numbers 1/2 (#37/38) 2007.

The Haworth Information Press®
An Imprint of The Haworth Press, Inc.

New York • London • Victoria (AU)
www.HaworthPress.com

Indexing, Abstracting & Website/Internet Coverage

This section provides you with a list of major indexing & abstracting services and other tools for bibliographic access. That is to say, each service began covering this periodical during the year noted in the right column. Most Websites which are listed below have indicated that they will either post, disseminate, compile, archive, cite or alert their own Website users with research-based content from this work. (This list is as current as the copyright date of this publication.)

Abstracting, Website/Indexing Coverage . . . . Year When Coverage Began

- *Combined Health Information Database (CHID)* 1994

- *Computer and Information Systems Abstracts <http://www.csa.com>* 2004

- *Current Cites [Digital Libraries] [Electronic Publishing]*
  [Multimedia & Hypermedia] [Networks & Networking]
  [General] <http://sunsite.berkeley.edu/CurrentCites/> 2000

- *EBSCOhost Electronic Journals Service (EJS)*
  <http://ejournals.ebsco.com> 2004

- *Educational Administration Abstracts (EAA)* 1991

- *Elsevier Scopus <http://www.info.scopus.com>* 2005

- *FRANCIS. INIST/CNRS <http://www.inist.fr>* 1997

- *Google <http://www.google.com>* 2004

- *Google Scholar <http://scholar.google.com>* 2004

- *Haworth Document Delivery Center*
  <http://www.HaworthPress.com/journals/dds.asp> 1989

- *IBZ International Bibliography of Periodical Literature*
  <http://www.saur.de> 1997

(continued)

- *Index Guide to College Journals (core list compiled by integrating 48 indexes frequently used to support undergraduate programs in small to medium sized libraries)* 1999

- *Index to Periodical Articles Related to Law <http://www.law.utexas.edu>*. 1992

- *Information Reports & Bibliographies* 1992

- *Informed Librarian, The <http://www.informedlibrarian.com>*. 1993

- *INSPEC is the leading English-language bibliographic information service providing access to the world's scientific & technical literature in physics, electrical engineering, electronics, communications, control engineering, computers & computing, and information technology <http://www.iee.org.uk/publish/>* 1989

- *Internationale Bibliographie der geistes- und sozialwissenschaftlichen Zeitschriftenliteratur . . . See IBZ <http://www.saur.de>* 1997

- *Journal of Academic Librarianship: Guide to Professional Literature, The* 1997

- *Konyvtari Figyelo (Library Review)* 2000

- *LABORDOC Library–Periodicals Section "Abstracts Section" <http://www.ilo.org>*. 2001

- *Library & Information Science Abstracts (LISA) <http://www.csa.com>* 1990

- *Library and Information Science Annual (LISCA) <http://www.lu.com>* 1998

- *Links@Ovid (via CrossRef targeted DOI links) <http://www.ovid.com>*. . . . 2005

- *Magazines for Libraries (Katz) . . . (see 2003 edition)* 2003

- *OCLC ArticleFirst <http://www.oclc.org/services/databases/>* 1990

- *OCLC ContentsFirst <http://www.oclc.org/services/databases/>* 1990

- *Ovid Linksolver (OpenURL link resolver via CrossRef targeted DOI links) <http://www.linksolver.com>*. 2005

- *PASCAL, c/o Institut de l'Information Scientifique et Technique. Cross-disciplinary electronic database covering the fields of science, technology & medicine. Also available on CD-ROM, and can generate customized retrospective searches <http://www.inist.fr>* 1997

- *Referativnyi Zhurnal (Abstracts Journal of the All-Russian Institute of Scientific and Technical Information–in Russian) <http://www.viniti.ru>* 2004

(continued)

- *REHABDATA, National Rehabilitation Information Center. Searches are available in large-print, cassette or Braille format and all are available on PC-compatible diskette <http://www.naric.com/naric>* **1998**

- *Scopus (Elsevier) <http://www.info.scopus.com>* **2005**

- *SwetsWise <http://www.swets.com>* **2001**

Special Bibliographic Notes related to special journal issues (separates) and indexing/abstracting:

- indexing/abstracting services in this list will also cover material in any "separate" that is co-published simultaneously with Haworth's special thematic journal issue or DocuSerial. Indexing/abstracting usually covers material at the article/chapter level.
- monographic co-editions are intended for either non-subscribers or libraries which intend to purchase a second copy for their circulating collections.
- monographic co-editions are reported to all jobbers/wholesalers/approval plans. The source journal is listed as the "series" to assist the prevention of duplicate purchasing in the same manner utilized for books-in-series.
- to facilitate user/access services all indexing/abstracting services are encouraged to utilize the co-indexing entry note indicated at the bottom of the first page of each article/chapter/contribution.
- this is intended to assist a library user of any reference tool (whether print, electronic, online, or CD-ROM) to locate the monographic version if the library has purchased this version but not a subscription to the source journal.
- individual articles/chapters in any Haworth publication are also available through the Haworth Document Delivery Service (HDDS).

To the memory of Bill Katz

Collection Development Issues in the Online Environment

CONTENTS

Introduction   1

COMMON ISSUES

Institutional Challenges to Increased Library Provision
   of Electronic Materials   3
    Gareth J. Johnson

Electronic Journal Delivery in Academic Libraries   15
    Stephen Crothers
    Margaret Prabhu
    Shirley Sullivan

Electronic Reference Works and Library Budgeting Dilemma   47
    Ibironke O. Lawal

Going E-Only: A Feasible Option in the Current UK Journals
   Marketplace?   63
    Martin Wolf

Are Electronic Serials Helping or Hindering Academic
   Libraries?   75
    Leila I. T. Wallenius

SPECIAL ISSUES

DMCA, CTEA, UCITA . . . Oh My! An Overview of Copyright
   Law and Its Impact on Library Acquisitions and Collection
   Development of Electronic Resources   83
    Leslie A. Lee
    Michelle M. Wu

Subscribing to Databases: How Important Is Depth and Quality
    of Indexing?   99
      Linwood DeLong

Annual Reports: Preserving and Disseminating a Source
    for Business History   107
      Cynthia L. Cronin-Kardon
      Michael Halperin

FUTURE ISSUES

Enhanced Online Access Requires Redesigned Delivery
    Options and Cost Models   119
      David Stern

Incentives for Deconstruction of the E-Journal   135
      Daniel E. Cleary

PDA Serials: Practical and Policy Issues for Librarians   145
      Stephen Good

Index   161

IN MEMORIAM

Dr. William (Bill) Katz passed away on September 12, 2004. Dr. Katz was Editor of the Haworth journals *The Acquisitions Librarian* and *The Reference Librarian* as well as *Magazines for Libraries*, *RQ* (the journal of the Reference and Adult Services Division of the American Library Association), and the "Magazines" column in *Library Journal*. In addition to his contributions to library science as an author and editor, he was a much-beloved professor in the School of Information Science and Policy at the State University of New York at Albany and a mentor to many of his former students in their professional lives. His association with The Haworth Press began in 1980 and lasted more than two decades. His steady hand, friendly guidance, and steadfast leadership will be missed by all of us at *The Acquisitions Librarian*, *The Reference Librarian*, and The Haworth Press.

ABOUT THE EDITOR

Di Su, MLS, MM, is Associate Professor and Head of Information Literacy at York College Library (CUNY). He has been a contributor to several publications, including *The Scribner Encyclopedia of American Lives*, *Biographical Dictionary of American Sports*, *Information Outlook*, and *The Reference Librarian*. Su was the editor of *Evolution in Reference and Information Services: The Impact of the Internet* (The Haworth Information Press, 2001). The book was praised as ". . . an inspiring and educational work for information students and veteran librarians alike" (*College & Research Libraries* 63, November 2002), "presents a fascinating assortment of viewpoints on the current state of electronic reference" (*Information Today* 20, March 2003), and "the book is highly recommended to anyone involved or interested in the provision of information services" (*Catalogue & Index* 148, Summer 2003).

Su earned his degrees at the University at Albany (SUNY), the University of Connecticut, West Virginia University, and the Shanghai Conservatory of Music. His research interests include the Internet, music, business and finance, and sports.

Introduction

In this digital age with the impact of the Internet, a vast amount of sources for research is being made available in electronic format. Some coexist with their print equivalent while others are in digital form only. Academic libraries routinely subscribe to electronic journals, electronic books, and other types of publications in electronic format. Electronic material has been quickly gaining popularity in a library's collection. Although the probability of a paperless library remains debatable, electronic material has become an inevitable issue to deal with for all the librarians in general, and for the acquisitions and collection development librarians in particular.

This book reflects the current practices in academic libraries, presents various viewpoints, offers suggestions, and attempts to be globally relevant. The contributors represent academic institutions in Australia, Canada, U.K., and U.S.A. The topics include advantages and disadvantages of e-material, accessibility and searchability, budgetary issues, copyright concerns, criteria of selection, database analysis, digital archiving and preservation, e-document delivery, e-material management and policies, future possibilities, and licensing options. The articles are grouped in three chapters: Common Issues, Special Issues, and Future Issues. It is hoped that this compilation will be informative and helpful to the readers. Nevertheless, due to the rapid change of technology, some facts might have already been out-of-date at the time this book is published. If that is the case, the book will at least serve the purpose of documenting the development for the given period.

[Haworth co-indexing entry note]: "Introduction." Su, Di. Co-published simultaneously in *The Acquisitions Librarian* (The Haworth Information Press, an imprint of The Haworth Press, Inc.) Vol. 19, No. 1/2 (#37/38), 2007, pp. 1-2; and: *Collection Development Issues in the Online Environment* (ed: Di Su) The Haworth Information Press, an imprint of The Haworth Press, Inc., 2007, pp. 1-2. Single or multiple copies of this article are available for a fee from The Haworth Document Delivery Service [1-800-HAWORTH, 9:00 a.m. - 5:00 p.m. (EST). E-mail address: docdelivery@haworthpress.com].

This work was supported (in part) by a grant from The City University of New York PSC-CUNY Research Award Program.

My thanks go to the contributors and the editorial staff at The Haworth Information Press. Also, my thanks go to my wife, Shaoshan Li, for her invaluable support and assistance. My gratefulness goes to the late Dr. Bill Katz who mentored me on this project through his last days.

Di Su

COMMON ISSUES

Institutional Challenges
to Increased Library Provision
of Electronic Materials

SUMMARY. The University of York is among the top universities in the United Kingdom, yet has not adopted all manner of electronic media. The University Library attempts to meet the demands placed upon it by its academic and student users for electronic media of all kinds, while working within a sometimes frame work that does not encourage exploitation of bleeding edge technologies. While pilot programs in electronic short loan have met with success, the University has yet to fully embrace a greater range of electronic materials provision. The acquisition of a virtual learning environment (VLE) may afford the Library the opportunity to develop

Gareth J. Johnson is Service Innovation Officer, Research & Innovation Unit, University of Warwick Library, Gibbet Hill Road, Coventry CV4 7AL, United Kingdom (E-mail: Gareth.Johnson@warwick.ac.uk).

[Haworth co-indexing entry note]: "Institutional Challenges to Increased Library Provision of Electronic Materials." Johnson, Gareth J. Co-published simultaneously in *The Acquisitions Librarian* (The Haworth Information Press, an imprint of The Haworth Press, Inc.) Vol. 19, No. 1/2 (#37/38), 2007, pp. 3-14; and: *Collection Development Issues in the Online Environment* (ed: Di Su) The Haworth Information Press, an imprint of The Haworth Press, Inc., 2007, pp. 3-14. Single or multiple copies of this article are available for a fee from The Haworth Document Delivery Service [1-800-HAWORTH, 9:00 a.m. - 5:00 p.m. (EST). E-mail address: docdelivery@haworthpress.com].

its hybrid collections further, and to overcome the reluctance of academic staff to embrace new technologies. *[Article copies available for a fee from The Haworth Document Delivery Service: 1-800-HAWORTH. E-mail address: <docdelivery@haworthpress.com> Website: <http://www.HaworthPress.com> © 2007 by The Haworth Press, Inc. All rights reserved.]*

KEYWORDS. Academic resistance, case study, electronic materials, library policy, United Kingdom, University of York

INTRODUCTION

We suffer an embarrassment of information riches today. Lecturers have a host of resources they can call upon, or would wish to, but rely on librarians to filter and present this information in an accessible way (Markland 2003). This is not a new problem, as can be seen in the introduction to *The Gentleman's Magazine* (Urban 1731), it was impossible to consult all the news sources of the day *"unless a man makes it his business to consult them all."* However, there remain significant challenges to the provision of resources within a budget and in a format appropriate to the institution, even when new technologies are taken into account.

How has this state of affairs arisen and more importantly how does the University Library play an effective role? In this article we will explore how this situation arose and the routes that are being adopted by the Library to manage and enable the delivery of electronic materials to its users. This article will look at the steps being taken at the University of York Library to provide access to electronic materials, and the particular challenges faced.

THE INSTITUTION

The University of York is located in the north of England and was founded in 1963 with only 200 students. This has since expanded to nearly 10,000 students and over 30 academic departments and research centres (University of York 2002 [1]). The University is officially rated among the top 10 Higher Education Institutions for both research and teaching in the UK (Quality Assurance Agency 2003, HERO 2002). The institution is based around a collegiate system, and departments have a great deal of autonomy in the way they operate. There are no faculties at York, with departments preferring to remain largely as islands of excellence. That is not to say there is not inter-departmental collaboration, although this arises through less formal channels than at other institutions. The J.B. Morrell University Library, where the author was based as of the writing of this article, supports teaching and research through a hybrid collection of materials (Johnson 2001). The Library manages purchases of resources on behalf of departments, guided by academic library representatives, and mediated and managed by a team of subject librarians.

THE SITUATION

Some institutions in the UK have taken the drastic step of moving to electronic journals only, scrapping all their print copies, freeing up their staff and shelf space. This is not the situation at the University of York where while increasingly subscriptions have been taken to online ejournals, there has yet to be a corresponding withdrawal of print materials. Academic departments are reluctant to take the plunge and shift to electronic only, preferring to keep a fall back print archive. Unfortunately the Library is reaching a point where a move to e-only access would allow the freeing of much needed shelf space. However, providing access to ejournals is only part of the story of e-materials. There are many issues surrounding other medias such as VLEs and ebooks that are a cause for concern for the Library.

York can be considered to be in an unusual position for a UK university (Maccoll 2001). While others such as Leeds and the Open University forge ahead with VLE developments, electronic short loans collections, and e-books, York seems caught in the backwoods providing virtually none of these particular resources centrally. That is not to say that no e-materials are provided for our users, with close to 3,000 full text electronic journals and around 50 databases available. Yet for a University virtually at the top of the UK league tables for teaching and research with some world-class departments this could be considered unusual.

The University's mission statement outlines its primary aim (University of York 2002[2]) to:

> provide an outstanding and distinctive intellectual, social, and physical environment in which research scholarship and learning may flourish, and all students and staff can achieve their potential.

That is to say an institution that strives to be unique and exceptional in all its operations–for York there is no second best. Departments are expected to achieve at the highest academic and research levels, with student entry requirements also correspondingly steep. However, these stringent entry requirements bring with them a high student expectation of opportunities and facilities that are not always fulfilled by the University's current resource provision. Academics have different needs, requiring specialised services unsuitable for the student population. Thus the Library is in the difficulty position of attempting to satisfy two disparate groups of users–academic researchers and tutors, and the student body, all within a finite budget.

STUDENT PERCEPTIONS

While there is anecdotal evidence for student dissatisfaction with some aspects of current e-material provision, in particular the lack of a campus wide VLE, this is a kind of service that cannot flourish without central intuitional support. The Library makes every effort to support innovations in teaching learning, but all too often is left floundering by institutional inertia preventing their introduction. Should a central VLE be introduced, the Library would almost certainly be heavily involved in its implementation, support, and usage for user education. However, there is a large body of positive response to the substantial e-journal provision which is reassuring for the Library. There has been little demand though for access to full-text e-books, although where these kinds of materials are available students have made quiet, and determined use of them. Hopefully this helps to assure the student body that considerations are being taken to provide these kind of materials, improving their perceptions of their University.

This perception of the University naturally impacts upon the Library service which wishes to be proactive in its service developments, rather reactive. The Library has, over the years been at the forefront of new ideas and developments at the University, such as VLE, electronic short loan, Web presence developments, and full-text e-materials. However, this desire to take advantage of such enabling systems has frequently been frustrated by the lack of University take up and more significantly central support and funding.

As the Library is very much in the front line of educational support we often hear directly from the student their perceptions of what the University is doing for them. In this respect student publications are useful to gather anecdotal evidence of user satisfaction levels. The Library also engages in service review questionnaires and focus groups. A total service review questionnaire is planned for spring 2004, and will no doubt reveal some useful information.

It should be noted that as the author works principally with the science departments, some of this article's perceptions could be attributed mainly to these kinds of users–as other reports have noted that the adoption of e-materials usage varies with academic discipline (Jackson Bartle & Walton 1999, Washington-Hoagland & Clougherty 2002). Those who are concerned with the adoption of e-materials by those in the humanities are directed to examine the findings of such projects as ARCHWay (Bower 2002), hosted here at York.

ELECTRONIC SHORT LOAN

A notable effect on the Library's part was the RALPHY electronic reserve project (Johnson 2000), a pilot initiated in 1996 and financed by University innovation funding, to explore the possibilities of providing key undergraduate reading list materials digitally. For three years this pilot service was moderately successful, on a small pilot scheme level, in the provision of these kinds of materials. Unfortunately the model used by the pilot was not easily scalable, without significant investment in staffing resources and copyright payments. Effectively this project was defeated by these spiralling copyright clearance costs, and the lack of additional available staff administration.

In the light of these problems, the managerial decision was taken to pursue more traditional print based short loan collection solutions in place of this scheme. In this decision York was not alone, but some projects have evolved into national services such as HERON based at Oxford, managing the copyright administration on behalf of their member institutions (Heron 2003, Pickering & Hughes 2001). Popular with lecturers and students alike, even today the author continues to be approached to enquire if it is possible to make teaching references available in this way. Until local VLE and portal developments are completed it is unlikely any kind of e-short loan collection will be re-evaluated. However, the positive publicity and liaison with academic staff involved with the project have been capitalised on, allowing closer working links with departments.

ELECTRONIC BOOKS

Electronic books are an area York has not adopted wholesale, though dialogues with e-book providers have taken place over a number of years. The position here could best be described as "ever watchful of the market," and indeed how other competing institutions are approaching the situation. Interestingly there has been virtually no demand at all from academic departments for the provision of these kinds of resources, and this more than any other aspect dictates the current Library position. Issues concerning the range and availability of appropriate texts (Green 2003) should also not be ignored as potential barriers to acceptance. There is certainly anecdotal evidence locally that users do not like to read long passages of text on the screen, and in many cases students are reluctant to pay for printing charges, currently more expensive than photocopying charges on campus.

If this disparity could be equalised there would be perhaps less reluctance on their part to use e-materials of all kinds. In some respects the increased availability of affordable mobile computers (PDAs and the like), may offer a level of portability equivalent to paper at a fraction of the cost to the end user, and potentially an upturn in the usage of e-materials.

Different licenses and publisher rules on access can also prove a significant barrier to use. If users experience difficulty in accessing print library books without accruing fines under a single system–how much harder will it be for them to comprehend the various rules that can apply to electronic book access from different providers? It may well be that these fears are unfounded, but it is possible that York's approach to the adoption only of mature technologies could avoid the teething troubles experienced by colleagues at other institutions in this area.

Perhaps the major reason e-books have not taken off at York is due to the lack of demand from departments. Some years ago the Library made overtures with *netLibrary*, with input from academics invited. As academics here have commented, while the idea of e-books is appealing the texts available are "not the right books for my teaching needs." Thus when the decision was made not to pursue e-books for this and other reasons, there was no outcries of dismay. The Library has however recently subscribed to the online *Encyclopaedia of Life Sciences*, *English Poetry Full Text Database*, and *Early English Books Online*, moves which have been cautiously welcomed by academics. Usage of these resources continues to be monitored to ensure that the expenditure is achieving a maximum benefit to the institution. Should any of them appear to be failing to reach their target audience then an promotional program will be instigated by the subject librarians to further educate the end users as to the benefits of these services.

VIRTUAL LEARNING ENVIRONMENTS

A range of different VLE systems have been used at York by dedicated individual academic staff members, but to date a centrally supported online learning environment service does not exist. A VLE would be an exciting opportunity to directly link e-materials with central course materials. The Library has been closely involved in one evaluation study of the *WebCT* system, while the author has been a member of the committee formulating an institutional online learning strategy. However, other than a generally raised awareness of the issues surrounding the implementation and use of managed learning environments by the participants little practical benefit has emerged. It should be noted though that the recent recruitment of a learning technologist could well prove a significant step forward for the University in the development of just such a central learning environment over the coming year. The University certainly has no intention of drastically falling behind, and the involvement with UK E-University Project is one way forward. The Grid and data curation is another area where libraries and librarians will be playing key roles in the coming year (Lyon 2003). York is part of the regional White Rose Consortium of Universities Grid project and this is one area where the J.B. Morrell Library and its staff will be playing an increasing role.

It has been the author's experience that while it is not explicitly stated as a policy, York does not adopt bleeding edge technologies. This unwritten policy can perhaps be adjudged shrewd in some respects. While other institutions fund initial developments, often struggling to find effective configurations through various experimental pilot schemes, York can take advantage of their findings when it finally adopts the mature technologies sometime later. Unfortunately the counterpoint to this is that at times it can be frustrating for academics and support staff alike that the University does not appear to be leading the way in this quarter, when it is at the forefront of so many other new developments such as the National E-University (UKeU 2003).

ACADEMICS AND E-MATERIALS

Turning to the other side of this article, that is persuading academics to make the decision to use, or in some cases switch to using, e-materials. Studies (Lawrence 2001) have shown that e-journal usage is higher than print, though at York a large body of resistance to change has been encountered in responses to the Library's efforts to persuade them to adopt these new mediums. This situation has been difficult to overcome, even with the subject librarians' considerable education and promotional programs. However, the Library's five-year strategy (Heaps 2001) states quite clearly that this is an area in which it wishes to develop:

> The University will continue to develop facilities which allow remote access from the desk-top in a rapid and convenient manner. . . It will also seek to evaluate, and if appropriate take advantage of other developments in information provision which may emerge over the period of the Strategy.

Speaking with these academics it emerges that there are a mixture of reasons behind this reluctance to switch. For some there are fears that a move to online only resources could leave the University a hostage to future fortunes. Again and again they ask "What happens if this publisher folds?" or "If we stop paying what rights do we retain to access the years we no longer have in print?" This question of long term validity of access has until recently prevented the Library taking advantage of some new electronic journal deals. However, provided the subject librarians continue to liase with their departments to allay unfounded fears it is possible that this difficulty can be worked around. York is now moving to take advantage of in-perpetuity back issue deals with Elsevier Science that may see a greater belief in stable access.

The other challenge we face is one of financial constraints. Departments are allocated a portion of the Library's information budget, based upon a model formula that takes into account various factors, and is used to pay for e-journal subscriptions. Other library funds exist to fund resources for all, including new innovations (e.g., e-books) at least in the initial instance. One option that the Library has explored, where allowable under licensing agreements, is to cancel print journals to free up funding for electronic journals. However, this is not an option that has met with initial widespread acceptance among some of our academic community.

In the coming year the Library will be exploring the electronic only access route as part of a pilot project to consider the reactions of all Library users to enforced e-access, and encourage them to make a greater use of e-journals. This step is born from the Library's current five-year strategy of moving towards a greater emphasis on accessibility of electronic full-text materials. The journals selected are already accessible electronically, but currently also available in print in the Library. The project intends to remove approximately 150 print journals, from the Library's open shelves. In this way it is hoped that users will modify their access habits. This project has been proposed and endorsed by the University Library committee, comprised of representatives from all academic departments and the situation will be closely monitored and evaluated at its conclusion. Whether electronic only access to journals forms the basis of the Library's future e-materials access policy remains to be seen.

As of this writing access to e-materials will shortly be streamlined, thanks to update work being performed upon the University's OPAC system (Aleph). Users will be able to simultaneously search across the print and e-print titles available, and seamlessly access them. The current situation, where a subsequent search of the Library's Web pages must follow an OPAC search has been the source of much frustration to our users. It is hoped this resolution will help them to view the e-journal only project in a more favourable light. Promoting the use of electronic resources is another aspect and is related to the cost effectiveness. Some institutions relish being experimental, but as mentioned above this is not York's standard operating practice. However, the Library has been able take some innovative steps like RALPHY, ARCH-Way, and E-Journal Only projects.

DEPARTMENT OF ELECTRONICS

One illustration on how the Library manages electronic materials policies would be to take the example of the Department of Electronics. Underpinning all of its working relationships with the Library is a departmental IRAP (Information Resource and Access Policy), agreed in consultation. Currently the department subscribes to the major journal packages from the IEEE and IEE, but has not been able to move to use the IEEE Explore Ejournal package. This is partially owing to cost implications, but there has also been significant reluctance over the past five years to explore this option at all, for reasons mentioned above. As of July-August 2003 the Library has arranged a trial access to IEEE Explore, with a goal of testing the water on this issue further.

With many of the other science departments there is a certain assumption that a move towards increased electronic accessibility would be favoured by the department. However, as in years previously the department has so far expressed continued concerns over long term access to archival journal issues if print subscriptions are terminated. This despite the fact that the IEEE could be considered a much safer option for long term access than other smaller publishing houses. There is also a fear that by moving to electronic only, the department would be effectively committing itself in perpetuity to accessing electronic journals only, tied into a deal they could not escape from with no print archive to fall back upon. However, the trial has been gathering a lot of popular acclaim from PhD students and junior researchers, for whom desktop access to e-materials is something they expect.

It should be noted that funding this move would be difficult. The department would have to cancel all of its print subscriptions to afford the package, something they remain reluctant to do. The Library awaits the result of this trial with considerable interest, as it could help inform our other efforts in this area.

CONCLUSIONS

There are many challenges ahead for the Library. Challenges in getting academics to change their usage patterns and students to access more resources. The future of Library provision of e-materials is likely to be tied in, at least for research purposes, with data roles such as the Grid. Individuals and departments remain the greatest barriers to electronic only policies, but through Library promotion, training, and trials of new systems this can be overcome.

By adopting a cautious, but watchful, approach to new technological innovations and e-material delivery methods, the University Library can benefit from the solutions to problems encountered by others. In this way we can ensure that our funds can be spent in the most effective manner, providing our users with a best possible service.

REFERENCES

Bower, G. 2002. *Archway: Gateway to resource sharing in archaeology* [online]. York: Archway Project, University of York Library, UK [cited 21 August 2003]. Available from World Wide Web: <http://www.york.ac.uk/services/library/archway/>.

Green, Maree. 2003. *Report of USTLG Summer Meeting on E-Books* [online]. University Science & Technology Librarians Group, UK, 2003 [cited 23 July 2003]. Available from World Wide Web: <http://www.leeds.ac.uk/library/ustlg/summer03/report.htm>.

Heaps, AEM. 2001. *Library Strategy 2000/1-2004/5* [online]. York: University Of York Library, UK, 2001 [cited 21 August 2003]. Available from World Wide Web: <http://www.york.ac.uk/services/library/libdocs/strategy0005.pdf>.

HERO. 2002. *Higher Education & Research Opportunities in the UK: RAE 2001: Results* [online]. Newcastle upon Tyne: HERO, Dickinson Dees, St Anne's Wharf, UK, 2002 [cited 21 August 2003]. Available from World Wide Web: <http://www.hero.ac.uk/rae/Results/>.

HERON. 2003. *HERON* [online]. Oxford: Heron, Ingenta, 2003 [cited 21 August 2003]. Available from World Wide Web: <http://www.heron.ingenta.com/>.

Jackson, M., Bartle, C., and Walton, G. 1999. Effective use of electronic resources. *Innovations in Education and Training International* 36: 320-326.

Johnson, Gareth J. 2000. R.A.L.P.H.Y.–The life and times of an electronic reserve project. *UKOLUG Newsletter* 11: 25-28.

Johnson, Gareth J. 2001. Issues and policy: Electronic journals strategies at the University of York *Information Services and Use* 21: 165-172.

Lawrence, Steve. 2001. Free online availability substantially increases a paper's impact. *Nature* 411: 521.

Lyon, L. 2003. eBank UK: Building the links between research data, scholarly communication and learning. *Ariadne* 36. Available from World Wide Web: <http://www.ariadne.ac.uk/issue36/lyon/>.

Maccoll, J. 2001. Virtuous learning environments: the library and the VLE. *Program* 35: 227-239.

Markland, M. 2003. Embedding online information resources in Virtual Learning Environments: Some implications for lecturers and librarians of the move towards delivering teaching in the online environment. *Information Research* 8: paper no. 158.

Pickering, H. and Hughes, J. 2001. HERON's role in copyright clearance for digital course readings. *ASSIGNation* 19: 31-35.

Quality Assurance Agency. 2003. *Quality Assessment Reports–University of York Index* [online]. Gloucester: Quality Assurance Agency for Higher Education, UK, 2003 [cited 21 August 2003]. Available from World Wide Web: <http://www.qaa.ac.uk/revreps/subjrev/institution_indexes/uni_of_york.htm>.

UkeU. 2003. *UKeUniversity Web Site* [online]. London: UKeUniversities World Wide Limited, Buckingham Gate, UK, 2003 [cited August 21 2003]. Available from World Wide Web: <http://www.ukeuniversitiesworldwide.com/>.

University of York [1]. 2002. *Operating Statement 2001/2* [online]. York: University of York, Planning Office, UK, 2002 [cited 28 July 2003]. Available from World Wide Web: <http://www.york.ac.uk/admin/po/opstat02.yrk/missionstatementandaims.htm>.

University of York [2]. 2002. *University of York: Overview* [online]. York: University of York, Communications Office, UK, 2002 [cited 21 August 2003]. Available from World Wide Web: <http://www.york.ac.uk/admin/presspr/misc/overview.htm>.

Urban, S. 1731. Introduction. *The Gentleman's Magazine* 1: 1.

Washington-Hoagland, C. and Clougherty, L. 2002. Faculty and staff use of academic library resources and services: A university of Iowa libraries perspective. *Portal: Libraries and the Academy* 2: 627-646.

Electronic Journal Delivery
in Academic Libraries

Stephen Crothers
Margaret Prabhu
Shirley Sullivan

SUMMARY. The authors recount experiences of the variety of problems and issues involved in providing access to electronic journals in a large academic library. The paper excludes concerns emanating from decisions to subscribe to aggregations such as those produced by vendors like EBSCO, but concentrates on scholarly journals ordered individually, or as part of a scholarly or scientific society package. Despite the number of years that publishers have been offering electronic journals, pricing policies are still fluid, and the problems of access encountered in the late 1990s still cause frustrating delays in provision of access to our academic staff and students. Questions on whether or not

Stephen Crothers is eJournal Administrator (E-mail: sjcrot@unimelb.edu.au); Margaret Prabhu is eJournal Administrator (E-mail: geetha@unimelb.edu.au); and Shirley Sullivan is Electronic Information Co-ordinator (E-mail: s.sullivan@unimelb.edu.au), all with the Department of Information Resources Access, University of Melbourne, Australia.

[Haworth co-indexing entry note]: "Electronic Journal Delivery in Academic Libraries." Crothers, Stephen, Margaret Prabhu, and Shirley Sullivan. Co-published simultaneously in *The Acquisitions Librarian* (The Haworth Information Press, an imprint of The Haworth Press, Inc.) Vol. 19, No. 1/2 (#37/38), 2007, pp. 15-45; and: *Collection Development Issues in the Online Environment* (ed: Di Su) The Haworth Information Press, an imprint of The Haworth Press, Inc., 2007, pp. 15-45. Single or multiple copies of this article are available for a fee from The Haworth Document Delivery Service [1-800-HAWORTH, 9:00 a.m. - 5:00 p.m. (EST). E-mail address: docdelivery@haworthpress.com].

Available online at http://www.haworthpress.com/web/AL
doi:10.1300/J101v19n37_03

15

to use a subscription agent to assist in solving these problems are raised. There are no hard and fast rules, and no easy answers. *[Article copies available for a fee from The Haworth Document Delivery Service: 1-800-HAWORTH. E-mail address: <docdelivery@haworthpress.com> Website: <http://www.HaworthPress.com> © 2007 by The Haworth Press, Inc. All rights reserved.]*

KEYWORDS. Academic libraries, accessibilities, Australia, scholarly electronic journals, subscription agents, University of Melbourne

INTRODUCTION

There are many decisions confronting libraries when they provide access to electronic journals. These are not limited to selection of content, but include technology, license, training and publicity issues. This paper considers scholarly journal titles ordered individually, omitting aggregations and the "Big Deal." Even with this narrow focus there is abundant scope for variety, as publishers reassess their subscription options on what sometimes feels like a daily basis. The paper will not be discussing training, publicity or license issues, as these are beyond the scope of activities undertaken by the ejournal administrators. The authors analyzed pricing convolutions entertained by publishers of scholarly journals, and the vagaries of access provisions in previous articles in 2001 and 2002. These are available at <http://www.alia.org.au/alj/50.4/full.text/electronic.journals.html> and <http://www.alia.org.au/alj/51.3/full.text/electronic.journals.html>.

ROLE OF EJOURNAL ADMINISTRATORS

The role of ejournal administrators varies from institution to institution. Founded in 1853, the University of Melbourne is one of Australia's leading research universities, with over 30,000 students in a broad range of disciplines. When the work first became necessary at the University in the mid '90s, one person, who also undertook a variety of other tasks, fulfilled this role. The work grew, however, in volume and complexity, with the growth in the electronic journal industry. Now, responsibility for electronic resources are shared between different personnel. Other staff (including collection managers) are responsible for establishing links from abstracting and indexing services to the full-text journals, systems maintenance, and license negotiation. The administrators share with other colleagues the e-resource acquisition and cataloging processes. The administrators' exclusive tasks include setting up electronic journal access, ensuring required passwords are available and monitoring sites for content changes. Arguably the most important and time consuming, however, is their role as a point of contact for users experiencing access difficulties.

The workload of the ejournal administrators shows no signs of diminishing in the foreseeable future. The authors had expected that the workload would diminish rather than expand as electronic provision of information became increasingly common over the past few years, but this has not eventuated. The provision of electronic access has become mainstream, as expected, but the means of ensuring access are still time consuming. It has proved impossible to create standard flowcharts to streamline the tasks involved in providing access. Each publisher or vendor has its own methods, and these remain fluid. Publishers are improving their processes and so are subscription agents, but there is a long way to go yet before electronic journals are integrated into workflows in the manner of print journals. As Rollo Turner notes, "The management of electronic titles calls for greater skills than was the case with print and so electronic journals are taking a much greater amount of professional staff time" (Turner).

> In spite of considerable efforts by libraries, agents and intermediaries to develop systems and ways of working to minimize costs it seems apparent to me that the cost of administration [sic] electronic journals is in fact far higher than that for purely paper journals, and higher still when both media co-exist. What is worse it appears to be growing. (Turner)

> Maintaining ejournal subscriptions and access . . . is not a function that is being done methodically here now–problems are dealt with as they are serendipitously discovered, but we don't have any method for systematically verifying that access is available (on an issue by issue level; of course we verify that we have access to new subscriptions, etc. (Harper)

ACTIVATION OF ONLINE JOURNAL ACCESS

Establishing access to electronic journals usually means registration at the publisher's site, providing the publisher with the institution's IP addresses, and liaising with the institution's systems staff to ensure the technical aspects work smoothly. "This can be time consuming and at times not especially straightforward" (Turner).

> I've been trying to identify the most time-consuming tasks for e-journal management and at the top of my list is (surprise, surprise!) the activation forms for institutional access to online journals. The major publishers have got reasonable systems for this but some make this process far too complicated. The worst problem is to do with the lack of recognition of Class B IP addresses. We have one IP address for the whole campus which looks something like this 176.111.*.* (this isn't our real one!) Very often we fill out all the details of our institution, administrator, administrator's username and password, name of administrator's cat, etc. and then finally try to enter the class B IP address only to find out it's not permitted in that format. Only class C or D addresses are accepted so all the information we've just typed in is lost. Then we spend ages trying to contact the publisher who then puts the class B IP address in for us manually (usually several days later). (Lewis)

Louise Cole from University of Leeds recounted her frustrations with the process in an e-mail to a UK based discussion list (Cole a). Cole's e-mail was answered by a number of other academic librarians agreeing with her views and relating their own experiences, such as Emma Hurcombe (Hurcombe).

Mieko Yamaguchi from Bangor mentioned that:

> If you were at Rollo Turner's workshop at the UKSG last week you will know that the problem of having to activate access to "online with print" subscriptions using those elusive subscription numbers came near the top of our "suggestions for improvement." I am beginning to think that "free online with print" is actually very expensive in terms of staff time both for libraries and subscription agents. It looks as if publishers are beginning to unbundle print and online and this would at least give us a choice as well as more clout when online access does not work (wishful thinking)! . . . (Yamaguchi a)

The problem used to be frequently encountered at the University of Melbourne, and one of the authors also responded to the e-mail recommending the use of subscription agents to ease the burden.

Our suppliers for eg: Swets Blackwell and DA Information Inc.
are particularly very helpful and have made our lives easier by entering our subscription nos. which is required for activating our
online access on their website which helps to a large extent . . .
(Prabhu)

Ingenta, a firm providing publishers with a web platform for their
journals, acquired CatchWord, a similar firm, in February 2001.
CatchWord subsequently was renamed Ingenta Select. Ingenta and
Ingenta Select now share the same content. Any previous content,
registration and subscription information accessed on CatchWord is
now accessible on Ingenta Select. Ingenta is a document delivery
service, offering access to its electronic publication collection and to
a larger database of publications. Ingenta Select offers access to only
the electronic collection. Ingenta Select also contains some books not
available on Ingenta. (Compiled from <http://www.Ingenta.com> and
<http://www.Ingentaselect.com>.) Confused? You are not alone. Li-
brary staff experience difficulty in knowing how to differentiate between Ingenta and Ingenta Select. Patrick Condron from the University
of Melbourne raised the following points:

I have noticed while doing my electronic journals page updating
today that CatchWord has been taken over by Ingenta and renamed Ingenta Select. Furthermore, we seem to be adding Ingenta
Select (or CatchWord) sites that are an exact copy of other records
we are adding for Ingenta sites. Reading on the Ingenta Select site,
they are looking to integrate the two services to one, I assume
Ingenta. Should we be removing any CatchWord records that have
duplicate Ingenta records or has a decision already been made on
this? (Condron b)

Louise Cole raised similar questions in an e-mail to the LIS E-journals list (Cole b). University of Melbourne has decided to provide access to the same title via Ingenta and Ingenta Select. This is part of a
deliberate policy to provide users with all possible avenues of access
through different platforms, given the notorious instability of electronic
access.

Ingenta Select in 2003 changed its website for institutional administrators by adding a new symbol beside each subscribed title:

§ indicates access to this title is enabled for the years specified. If you have a current subscription and wish to extend access to this title please contact support@Ingentaselect.com including your CID number, journal title and subscription number. (<http://www. Ingentaselect.com/cgi-bin/sub_act.pl>)

The result is that both Ingenta and Ingenta Select send out e-mails such as the following:

We have received your request to enable access to the Veterinary Anaesthesia and Analgesia. However, this could not be set due to the following reason : We have been unable to locate your institution within the files sent to us by the publisher. Please provide us with any payment/reference details that relate to your subscription so we can contact the publisher for verification. (<subscriptions@Catchword.com>)

Claire Hill, Customer Support Administrator at Ingenta, revealed that, "The activation form is used to request access to a title, but we were finding that subscribers were requesting access multiple times causing duplications on accounts" (Hill a).

One of the authors suggested that, when titles are already registered, publishers could forward the new customer number to Ingenta and the ejournal administrators. Another suggestion the author made is for a web-based form to enable the institutional administrator to update information about previously registered titles, such as customer numbers. Claire Hill replied:

Depending upon the publisher and how access is enabled some publishers are able to change the customer number but a large number will provide you with a publisher account number that should not change. Your suggestion is a very good one and one that has been raised before but we will still have the problem of duplicate entries for titles. We are also starting to bulk load agent subscription files for Swets and Ebsco which will streamline the process. We are looking to improve the activation system this year and this will hopefully make things a lot easier. (Hill b)

Some publishers, subscription agents, and aggregators are starting to identify titles available for institutional access via online journal websites. Ingenta and Ingenta Select do not maintain a current listing, as Stacy Pober, Information Alchemist at the Manhattan College Library, discovered:

> Some journals offer free online access for print subscribers through the Ingenta service. Does anyone know how to get a listing on the Ingenta site of those titles for which we get 'institutional access'? I'm pretty sure there used to be a way to drill down into the site and display this, but either I've forgotten the meandering path of clicks or they've eliminated this option. (I'm going to e-mail them, and I know that they'll be able to e-mail me a report of our subscribed titles–but web access would be really nice.) (Pober)

Publishers, aggregators, subscription agents, and libraries are still attempting to understand each other's electronic roles and policies. It is encouraging to see some improvement in communication and understanding. Most University of Melbourne journal subscriptions are placed through subscription agents. Negotiating with major publishers for access to the electronic component of bundled titles is becoming less difficult. Most online registration forms and account details are now easier to understand and process than was the case approximately five years ago. Institutional administrators can activate the online component and keep the account details up to date on major publishers' web-based registration forms. Difficulties, however, still arise, especially when a subscription agent places a print subscription bundled with electronic access from a small publisher which maintains its own ejournal website. The division of responsibilities between the agent and the library can cause confusion. Often the small publisher has already entered subscription agent details on the registration form. This necessitates communication to the publisher by the institutional administrator requesting that details of the institutional administrator replace those of the agent, so that control of the online component of the journal subscription can remain in the hands of the institutional administrator. These problems and more are demonstrated in the following e-mail to Institutional Investor:

> The University of Melbourne has a number of subscriptions to journals which you publish. These are ordered through our subscription agent, Swets Blackwell. The subscriptions to the journals include both print issues sent to us by mail and electronic access which you kindly provide from your web site. These titles include: Journal Of Derivatives, Journal Of Portfolio Management, Journal

Of Fixed Income, Journal Of Structured And Project Finance. The first issue is that we are confused about our account. Last year, an account was established under the username: one and one23 (not our real username and password). Originally the account was listed as Swets Blackwell Inc., Exton PA, USA. We thought we had changed the account details to Melbourne University with our Australian address. Is it possible that this account is not recognised as our account but as Swets Blackwell's? What appears to have caused our current confusion is our query through Swets Blackwell about electronic access to the Journal of Fixed Income. Your reply mentions account no. 12345678 (not our real account number). Are these two separate accounts as the journal lists are different? "My account" page for the 12345678 account lists the journals as Real Estate Finance, Journal Of Alternative Investments, Journal Of Derivatives, Journal Of Fixed Income, Journal Of Investing, Journal Of Portfolio Management, Journal Of Risk Finance, Journal Of Structured And Project Finance. While "My account" page for our one23 account lists our journals as Journal Of Derivatives, Journal Of Investing and the Journal Of Portfolio Management. The second issue is that as you can note, both "My account" lists titles that according to our records, we do not have any subscriptions for. Is it possible after resolving our account situation for these titles to be removed? (Crothers a)

Despite numerous e-mails from the authors and from the subscription agent, the problems with this publisher have been ongoing for the past six months or so. No sign of resolution appears on the horizon.

TROUBLESHOOTING

As Duranceau remarks, "If a library offers e-resources, then without a doubt it needs staff to troubleshoot inevitable access problems" (Duranceau, 319). Problems associated with access denials can be caused by subscription breakdown, incorrectly setting up the access requirements, errors on the part of the publisher, or a host of other reasons. Finding what has gone wrong and correcting the fault can take a considerable length of time (Turner).

A loss of access to the journal *Genetics* was brought to our attention by an academic staff member. "We seem to have lost our online subscription to the journal Genetics. Is this correct or a temporary error?"

(Andrianopoulos). This was a case where we maintained a current subscription to the title, but the publisher wanted proof of payment from our subscription agent before restoring online access. Another query from an academic in one of our psychiatric centers asked, "Could you please advise the current status of the university's subscription to the British Journal of Psychiatry? BJP via Highwire informs that the sub expired January 30" (Troy). One of the authors e-mailed the publisher and access was rapidly restored, with apologies.

While one of the authors was activating institutional access to a Walter de Gruyter title, she discovered that all the links previously created for our other Walter de Gruyter English language titles were linking to the German language titles. All the links had to be updated so that they led once more to the English language titles. We had no notification of the changes in URLs from the publisher or subscription agent. Colleagues from other countries relate similar experiences. Lesley Crawshaw, from the University of Hertfordshire, noted that one recurring problem is when the syntax of the URL changes completely without prior warning from the relevant publisher. These problem URLs are mainly found by accident when checking the URL for a new title and she pleads, "We understand the need for change, we just like to find out about it in advance, not from our users or by accident" (Crawshaw 2002).

A problem Crawshaw related about accessing a title through Ingenta Select (Crawshaw 2003a) provoked a flood of responses on the LIS E-Journals discussion list providing further examples supporting Crawshaw's points. These include e-mails from Peter King (King), Graham Stone (Stone), and Carol Morse (Morse).

A staff member from Ingenta, monitoring the list, was quick to respond to the list explaining the problems which are causing the various difficulties raised by the librarians on the list, and outlining what Ingenta is doing to solve the problems (Meddings).

A flurry of e-mails related to problems gaining access to Aslib titles when they moved to the Emerald site. (See item 5 on the April 2003 archives at <http://www.jiscmail.ac.uk/lists/lis-e-journals.html>.) But sadly,

> Still no access to the Aslib titles we subscribe to online, and Aslib tell us our passwords are the ones which should work, and asked us to 'try again.' This has now been going on for a while, and clearly we wouldn't report a problem if there wasn't one . . . E-mailing in the hope that someone will get this sorted for us, and again flagging up to lis-e-journals subscribers that this group of titles are a pain to administer! (Cole c)

Emerald responded on 1st May by assuring librarians that the obstacles they are encountering will be removed.

> Those of us who have been raising problems with the ever-changing usernames and passwords required to access Aslib subscriptions through Emerald on this list recently will be pleased that a solution to all our frustrations is near at hand. It demonstrates the value of this list in trying to get shared problems resolved to our mutual satisfaction. I would also like to thank Aslib and Emerald for working to get this problem resolved. (Crawshaw 2003b)

PUBLISHERS OR AGENTS FOR SUBSCRIPTIONS

> Has anyone looked recently into the economics/advantages and disadvantages of using a subscription agent for a journal collection of about 60 titles? For those who handle everything directly with each journal publisher: does it prove time-consuming? Has anyone changed recently and why? (Kewley)

"Even though it is more work for you, in some cases it is much better in terms of customer service to deal directly with the publisher" (Oster). Dianne Oster's comment, although not in response to the above query by Kewley, is included here as a dissenting view to the majority opinion. Comments from a poll on use of subscription agents initiated by *Infotoday* at <http://www.infotoday.com/default.shtml> in March 2003 include the following:

- We used to use an agent but the financial outlay did not justify the work involved in trying to get them to act on our behalf. As we have a small number of titles, we now order all direct from the publishers and have had less angst and more money. For those who subscribe to a large number of titles using an agent makes sense and saves a lot of time; one just has to ensure one selects a reliable and active agent.
- We will continue to use a subscription agency because handling subscriptions individually would overwhelm library staff and the college's accounts payable person.
- Have you tried to order/maintain dozens of journals individually?
- Are the people who voted no going to add on more staff to deal with all of the publishers?

As of March 10th, 2003, the responses were 71% in favor, and 29% against using subscription agents.

> It remains a wonder why many of the publishers who give online access via their own site are unable to communicate internally efficiently (and with other service providers) and set up access to titles that they know we subscribe to. . . . Generally, tallying up lists and online subscriptions with publishers or service providers is an impossible task. We have a go every now and then, when staff time permits, but rarely (never!) get to the point when everything is correct. Before sending this e-mail, I thought I would just check the title Lesley mentions [in an e-mail to LIS-E-Journals dated 11 April 2003], Journal of sports science, as this is one we have just started subscribing to. We have set up an online link via Swetswise, our agent, and had not bothered with Metapress because of the problems with them, so I assumed everything was ok. However, I've just discovered that Swetswise have linked directly to metapress who have not set up our access!!! AAHHH! (Morris 2003b)

And from an Australian colleague,

> We had a poor experience dealing directly with Taylor & Francis. Our problems were mainly related to issues of invoicing and failure on their part to keep track of payments and what they should be applied to. Similar problems occurred with this publisher in other parts of the University as well as the Library. I have stopped dealing directly with T & F and placed our orders for their titles through an agent. Having said that I think the problems may be because T & F do not have a business office in Australia, do not understand Australian tax requirements, and seem to stumble on exchange rates. In a country with a local office this may not be a problem at all. (Dartnall)

Taylor & Francis, like other publishers and vendors, maintains a presence on various e-mail discussion lists, and was quick to reply to the various complaints about lack of communication as well as the technical difficulties recounted on the list. They explained their efforts to communicate and ended by giving contact details for anyone wanting to get in touch (Thompson). Their staff certainly proved helpful to University of Melbourne staff working with the subscription agent to identify and re-establish access to problematic titles. The following e-mails forwarded from the subscription agent explain how to go about activating access to titles available through MetaPress.

On 5th February they wrote:

> Thank you for your e-mail–of course, here follows the process we advise customers to take in order to gain online access: The customer will need to visit http://taylorandfrancis.metapress.com where they can register for access. . . .When registering as an institution . . . the administrator will need choose an institution code (a short identifier max of 10 characters, chosen to represent the institution). For customers desiring IP recognition there is also the opportunity to input these addresses along with their main details. For those registering as an institution there are two ways to arrange access–they may e-mail online@tandf.co.uk with a list of the journals to which they subscribe and subscriber numbers, I will then manually arrange and verify these. Or there is the option to 'assert' their own access to journals without contacting us the publisher–we will check for paid subscriptions in arrears. To do this customers will need to choose the 'Activate Access' option in the content menu and click on 'Select Access,' then browse for journals using the search facilities. By ticking the box next to a title and clicking 'apply changes' at the top or bottom of the page they can then view immediately.

And an e-mail from the following day gave further explanations:

> Customers would not need to use their subscriber number literally on the website, as we will search for payment using the institution name and address provided upon registration. If we really cannot find proof of a valid subscription in this way, we will then contact the customer to ask for an agents reference or TandF reference to pinpoint the correct account. When asserting access, some customers may get confused with the second Activate Access option–which is to provide an Access Activation Code. They often assume their sub number or agents ref should work here, however this facility is not in use and as we cannot tailor it to our customers needs at present we are pushing Metapress to remove it from the website.

As the e-mails indicate, it is not all smooth sailing. As implied above, at the University of Melbourne, sometimes we deal directly with publishers, but sometimes we engage the services of one of our subscription agents as an intermediary. The working life of ejournal coordinators frequently can be eased by assistance from subscription agents we believe. As an example, to establish access to the online component of the *International Journal of Epidemiology*, we initially approached the publisher directly about our access problems, but brought in our local subscription agent, DA Information Services, when the publisher required payment details. The agent followed up on this and also thoughtfully supplied a list of other titles supplied through them by that publisher.

A less successful occasion when we used a subscription agent was when we placed a new order for the print and online access for *Human Molecular Genetics* but were unable to access the title. The agent replied to our request as follows:

> I understand that access will be halted and all print issues will also be on hold for now, as there's some payment confusion with regards to our payment to OUP. We are definitely trying to speed up and clear up any misunderstanding/miscommunication between Swets Blackwell and OUP, and will update you as soon as possible. We regret that this is causing much inconvenience on your end, and realize that this is an important publication for your institution and will endeavour to solve this problem as soon as we can. (Gacek)

Turner cannot be considered a disinterested observer; nonetheless, the comments he makes are borne out by the experience of many ejournal administrators. "This situation is made doubly difficult for both library and agent when publishers refuse to deal with agents for the electronic content, even when their customers require them to do so" (Turner).

> And as more libraries go online only, I think it becomes more important to have online subscriptions managed by agents whose years of experience benefit us all. For example, I need management reports that encompass all of our subscriptions. Separate reports from each publisher would be less effective and more labor intensive since we would have to compile them ourselves. And let's not forget one of the original needs solved by the subscription agents–aggregated renewals! It appears to me to be more efficient for subscription agents and publishers to resolve any problems

with the process of online subscription management so that we all can continue with successful business relationships based on our various niches of expertise. (Corbett)

Given the reality of the workflow in most institutions, most publishers seem to realize that they are shooting themselves in the foot if they won't allow clients to utilize jobbers. Even so, some of them have deduced that we have no choice but to pay the higher subscription price for that "luxury." (Blackwell)

Over the years we have had several publishers refuse to deal with a jobber. The reasons varied, but the end result was the same: order directly or do without the journal. I don't believe that this is a trend; I believe that it's the publisher's wish to eliminate, perhaps, the jobber's percentage in an already tight economy. (Eastland)

For further comments on this theme, see the archives of <liblicense-l@lists.yale.edu> for the month of June 2003, especially the e-mail from Richard Jasper (Jasper) and Peter Picerno (Picerno).

Chuck Hamaker from the University of North Carolina Charlotte asked for clarification on whether or not Elsevier allows electronic subscriptions to be handled through agents. Goldstein replied that she was informed by Elsevier that they do not allow libraries to go through vendors for electronic only access (Goldstein). Niles, however, responded:

That has been our understanding, but a colleague from our Health Sciences library told me recently that Elsevier will allow the electronic access charges to be handled by vendors, if the customer specifically requests (demands?) that it be that way. (Niles)

Daviess Menefee responded on behalf of Elsevier with the following heartening news:

. . . Elsevier has taken the position to work directly with customers who purchase the electronic version of their journals. This policy has been consistent since the introduction of ScienceDirect in 1998. Over the course of time, however, some libraries asked Elsevier to allow invoicing and payment via agents for electronic products. Elsevier has agreed to this process provided there is mutual consent by all parties beforehand and a single subscription agent is involved. For print formats, Elsevier continues to work with subscription agents and encourages libraries to maintain their agent relationships for print delivery. (Menefee a)

This is fortunate, as

> librarians worldwide report a lack of responsiveness from Elsevier; failure to meet terms of agreements; inability to respond to title level access problems; lack of follow up on routine queries; sloppiness and intransigence if not neglect in responding in a timely fashion during contract negotiations. So pervasive are these experiences that the goodwill created by the online system, the platform and content, has been seriously diluted even though few librarians consider these behaviors as "personal." They see it as the price of doing business with a monopoly service. (Hamaker a)

For some detailed accounts of difficulties librarians have experienced with Elsevier, and Elsevier's responses to their challenge to respond, see posts by Phil Davis (P. Davis), Daviess Menefee (Menefee b), Chris Baumle (Baumle), Chuck Hamaker (Hamaker b), Bruce Abbott (Abbott), and Bernd-Christoph Kaemper (Kaemper c) on the Reed Elsevier discussion list during March 2003 <reedelscustomers@lists.cc.utexas.edu>.

PRICING ISSUES

A 2002 survey by Swets Blackwell on electronic journal policy states that more publishers than in previous years have changed, or plan to change, their pricing model (Morris 2002).

> Perhaps one of the most uneven, confusing and frustrating phenomena facing publishers and subscribers is how to charge for electronic journals. Different publishers are exploring the marketplace to see what makes sense and how to protect their revenue streams from declining print sales. The frustrating area for libraries and consumers is that these varying pricing algorithms often do not make sense or are unnecessarily linked to the print product, whether one wants to receive it or not. (ASA 2002)

Pinfield commented back in 2001 that "the criteria on which pricing models should be based for all electronic products is still very unclear.

Should price be based on use? If so, how is use determined? Should it be based on size of user community? If so, how is size calculated?" (Pinfield). Publishers are still experimenting with pricing. For example, the *British Dental Journal* bundled print and online till 2001. In 2002, the publisher changed the policy to require a surcharge for the online component if required with a print subscription. In 2003, online access is once more bundled with a print subscription.

A query regarding restricted online access bundled with the print subscription to the Australian scholarly society journal, *Anaesthesia and Intensive Care*, obtained the following response:

> The issue of single computer access to institutions is only temporary until such time as pricing and administration issues have been established. Our subscribers will then be further advised. Apologies for any inconvenience, but for the time being access to the AIC website will only be available via a single computer, the IP address of which is captured when the application is submitted. We will try to rectify this as quickly as possible and will keep you advised. (Conolly)

In 2003, Blackwell Publishing has the following purchasing options besides consortia deals for institutions. These are premium subscription with extended online access, standard subscription with standard online access, and online only subscription. For details, see the website at <http://www.blackwellpublishing.com/cservices/pricelist.pdf>. The Royal Society of Chemistry offers journal packages offering print only, print plus online and online only at <http://www.rsc.org/is/journals/current/jpricing.htm>. After consulting widely with its customer groups, OUP developed a two-stage approach to the new pricing model based on FTE. The 2004 institutional price list along with the pricing policy and conditions are available at <http://www.oupjournals.org/prices>.

> I wonder if others who access this list have had the same impression as me, which is that pricing models seem to be getting more complicated. There are good reasons for this. I suspect that publishers (like OUP in this instance) are actually listening to librarians and what they say they want, but they are getting differing feedback. At one time publishers (in my experience) tended to be more interested in what competitors were doing and in the early days of online that tended to mean that every company came up with more or less the same solution. In practice from a library

viewpoint is the emergence of a range of models a good thing or a bad thing? Does it enable customers to choose what suits them or does it just complicate their lives? (Watkinson)

I've had e-mails from OUP about a banded pricing structure for online access, which will depend upon organisational size. I subscribe to several specialist clinical journals. There are only ever going to be perhaps 20-30 FTEs on my sites interested in the titles, due to the small nature of the clinical teams. To determine pricing according to the size of the whole organisation is as relevant–and as fair–as pricing according to readers' hair colour. The organisational FTE is not a relevant criteria to use. Organisations differ widely in the make-up. A large, single-focus research organisation will have far more readers for a specialist journal than a generalist organisation like us. The only way I can see that organisational FTE is relevant is a rather cynical assessment of the ability to pay higher charges. Does anyone else have any views on this. Has anyone else complained to the OUP? (Roddham)

FTE models of pricing frequently cause anguish, especially for large institutions. Institutional pricing models of scholarly society publishers are often driven by fear of membership losses and represent extraordinary increases to current library expenditures (French). For example, the pricing models of the American Geophysical Union (AGU) (based on numbers of doctorates awarded by each campus)

for electronic access alone result in costs more than twice current expenditures by UC libraries on print versions of the journals and there are no discounts on print subscriptions. Some major institutions with significant geology programs immediately announced they would not license AGU journals at these prices. The CDL communicated to the AGU disappointment with the pricing but continued to pursue other essential requirements (e.g., verifying that the content is complete, investigating mechanisms for linking at the article level to indexes). AGU has now agreed that UC could sign a single license for all campuses. (French)

Since that exchange, the AGU has responded further to complaints about an unrealistic pricing policy. Louise Cole from Leeds forwarded information to the LIS-E-Journals list in mid June 2003:

I thought you would be interested in the following message from AGU on institutional access to its e-journals, given the problems libraries have been having with the pricing policy. As you see, it was only announced last Wednesday, and as far as I can see, has not been circulated on library/HE lists.

Louise

Date: 11 Jun 2003

Subject: new AGU subscription options announced

Greatly expanding the number of institutions that have full electronic access was identified as a top priority by both the Council PRC and the PubsCom. A strategy for building subscriptions is the introduction of "per-user rates." Today, we began notifying libraries about this new option and about the opportunity for qualifying institutions to add titles for a very modest annual access fee. Institutions with active licenses of any kind were sent an e-mail message telling them about these options. You can find the information about the options at http://www.agu.org/pubs/Institution_options_2003.html

Judy C. Holoviak
Deputy Executive Director and
Director of Publications
AGU (Cole e)

Because Cell Press relies heavily on individual subscriptions, its institutional prices for an online subscription have reflected expected loss of these subscriptions and are determined, apparently, on a case-by-case basis (French). Prices will be based on an undisclosed formula that is FTE based and depends on the number of academic staff and graduate students in biomedical sciences, including chemistry and biology, excluding health sciences (Hamaker a).

The UC libraries expressed willingness to consider a quote for systemwide access to the five Cell Press titles that is roughly two and one-half times greater than the collective expenditures on print, subject to the opportunity to verify that the personal subscriptions upon which the quote is based are those of UC individuals. Unfortunately, Elsevier will not, after repeated requests over several months, supply this information. It is impossible to validate the assumptions of potential individual subscription loss with no information on how the numbers are derived. In checking with other libraries we have found some prominent institutions resisting licensing Cell Press titles for similar reasons. (French)

Christine Orr passed on to the Chemistry discussion list the following information supplied by Thomas von Foerster of the American Institute of Physics.

This year, in response to requests from librarians for notification of our tiered prices, we have accelerated our procedures for setting and disseminating subscription prices for journals published by the American Institute of Physics. . . . We are grouping institutions into five tiers, based on fair, consistent, and objective criteria that measure research activity relevant to our journals, using current and historical data readily available to AIP. . . . For additional details on AIP's 2004 pricing . . . please visit http://librarians.aip. org/tiers.html. All subscription rates, including the multi-journal packages and combination offers, will be posted at that URL <http://www.aip.org/journal_catalog/institutions.html> by early June. (Orr)

GRACE PERIOD

As academic staff are becoming more amenable to electronic-only access to journals, ensuring smooth, reliable and transparent access is more important than when there was print backup. Swets Blackwell is one of the subscription agents working to persuade publishers to adopt 'grace periods' for electronic journals as they have allowed for print, so that access is not switched off on the 1st of January each year. Publishers have also been encouraged to process electronic journal renewals much more swiftly. The aim is to ensure that access continues uninterrupted, even if there are outstanding queries on pricing, payment, licensing, or other matters (Bley). The Association of Subscription Agents is also a key player and is calling for publishers to allow a grace period. The text of its call, including a code of good practice and a list of publishers granting a grace period at renewal time, may be found at <http://www.subscription-agents.org/egrace.html>.

The Divine/RoweCom debacle in 2003 has focused attention on the need for a grace period; for example,

> The Society for General Microbiology will extend its normal grace period to the end of March 2003 for both print and on-line versions of their journals for Divine/RoweCom subscribers. The situation will then be reviewed. (Noble)

But even prior to this, many publishers were realizing that it is necessary to allow a grace period for electronic subscriptions, as they do for print subscriptions. For example, "This is to confirm that OECD's standard policy is to grace electronic access for three months at the end of any subscription period" (Green) and "PNAS is pleased to announce the gracing of online access for institutional subscribers until March 6, 2003, as well as 2003 print issues 1, 2 and 3 for direct-ship customers" (Martin).

There are certain anomalies, however, as Crawshaw reports discovering:

> . . . that the grace periods from some publishers didn't always extend to the electronic version. . . . What we need are consistent grace periods otherwise this is another area of potential confusion for those of us trying to maintain access to our ejournals from year to year. Surely the grace period must apply to both the print and electronic versions of the journal, as in many cases we are paying extra for the privilege of online access. (Crawshaw 2003c)

She discusses a concrete example in an e-mail dated 11th April 2003 (Crawshaw 2003d) and Frank Norman provides an example from a scientific society publisher (Norman).

But a grace period would not necessarily solve the problem of loss of access–merely delay it.

> I would be interested to know if we are alone in our experiences with ASCE online journals. For the third time after 2001 and 2002, we have lost online access to our package of ASCE journals. On-line Service has been interrupted since April 1, 2003. This time, we received an early warning on March 12 (ASCE Online subscription alert) that our subscriptions had not been renewed. On receipt of this alert, our library, in cooperation with our subscription

agency, writing in parallel, immediately provided the publisher with all details of our subscription and payment, including a copy of the processed check which was faxed in mid March. Payment had already been made in mid November 2002, and the cheque had been cashed in early December. We urged the publisher to ensure that online access to our subscriptions would continue uninterrupted. If there is a perennial mystery that baffles acquisition librarians it is that every year again payments made through agencies don't show up in publisher's records. No amount of grace period seems to help, it's only effect being that problems show up later in the year. This time at least we received an early warning, and we were optimistic enough to assume that our immediate reaction could avoid interruption of online service for our patrons on campus. Alas, ASCE did not bother to follow up our e-mail exchange, and in the second week of April, we were alerted by one of our patrons that online access had been cut off. We claimed again and asked to restore online access immediately. No response so far! We are now contemplating to ask for some refund of our subscription money if online access is withheld any further. Have other libraries had similar experiences? (Kaemper a)

Rani Sinha responded with a similar tale to tell (Sinha).

I can report that–with the kind intervention of AIP's Online journal services who are hosting ASCE's journals and requested ASCE to urgently settle the matter–we had access only one day after my message to liblicense-l. In compensation for the several weeks we were cut off from access, we will ask for a partial refund or at least a voucher to be applied to purchases of other ASCE publications. Our requests to the publisher for comments, explanations or advice how such a situation could be avoided in future went unanswered, as in the previous years. (Kaemper b)

COMMUNICATION FROM PUBLISHERS

Poor communication from publishers to librarians is a recurring issue on e-mail discussion lists, with examples that make one wince. The various e-mails concerning the pricing policies of the American Medical Association, for example, are indicative of confusion caused by poor

communication practices. See, for example, the e-mails from Mark
Funk (Funk), Louise Cole (Cole d) and Lesley Crawshaw (Crawshaw
2003e).

> In the case of the ACM Digital Library the information on their
> site for librarians is appalling or non-existent. I did receive a reply
> to a recent e-mail I sent to them about this, but unfortunately it
> didn't answer the questions posed. (Crawshaw 2002)

> Has anyone experienced the frustration of patrons going to a jour-
> nal website and getting the message. "Institution subscription ex-
> pired in Jan. 2003"–when your institution NEVER had a print
> subscription or online access to the journal. Some patrons think we
> just forgot to pay a bill. Have there been any attempts to get pub-
> lishers to use language that is less misleading–more uniform. It is a
> PR issue–but it can be a significant one. (Paldan)

This e-mail provoked an immediate heartfelt response.

> Diane, you have hit one of my "hot" buttons! I have been ex-
> tremely unhappy with the language publishers/providers are using
> such as you describe in your message. Our library has had several
> instances where we DID have a subscription and had properly reg-
> istered for online access; there was simply a problem at the pub-
> lisher's end coordinating the access. Some of our faculty become
> quite incensed when they receive a message that the "subscription
> expired." The assumption is always that we cancelled the sub-
> scription and the library is to blame. Or is that what publishers
> want our patrons to believe? At least one time the message ap-
> peared after a trial was over–we NEVER had a subscription that
> could expire. Yet again, the library was being challenged to renew.
> And I had to spend several hours researching the whole situation to
> discover that there was never a subscription in the first place. I re-
> ally wish that publishers would find some more library-friendly
> language for these messages. There are enough instances when the
> problem is at the publisher's end that the declarative "your sub-
> scription has expired" is simply incorrect. How about: "You are
> currently not entitled to access this material. There are several rea-
> sons why this may be so. Please contact your library/site adminis-
> trator for further assistance." (S. Davis)

George Porter points out that, while the IEEE has not done a very good job of publicizing it, it is providing almost all of the information needed to provide good access to the materials in IEL. He elaborates in an e-mail dated 15th May 2003 (Porter). IEEE responded to this e-mail from Porter thanking him, and then detailing all the library support services they offer (Spada).

> With so many publishers adding additional backfiles sometimes free for existing subscribers, sometimes for a one-off charge, it is getting increasingly difficult to keep up with all the changes, especially when publishers don't tell us, their customers, about what they are up to. . . . Do you know that Annual Reviews, Inc. has now digitized all the backfiles of the Annual Review series, which can now be purchased for a one-off price of $5000 per location? I've known that this was in process for quite a while now, and had e-mailed Annual Reviews, Inc. back in the middle of September 2002, asking for further details, e.g., would this cost extra, etc. As we have print/online subscriptions to 22/29 Annual Reviews, I might have expected that the publisher might e-mail me (as the online subscription administrator), that the digitization of their backfiles was complete and provide me with pricing/license details. I had been promised that they would let me know once the backfile program was available. Maybe they've sent it on a flier, but e-mail to the designated contact seems to be the most sensible route of communicating such information. It was only because I was looking for an article in the Annual Review of Astronomy and Astrophysics that I spotted additional volumes that weren't there previously. I don't know how long it has been since the digitization has been completed and pricing available. Those of you who don't already know about it–did anybody?–can find further information at <http://www.annualreviews.org/inst-subscribers/ebvc.asp>. (Crawshaw 2003f)

Alerting services for librarians can range from the extremely useful to the problematic or non-existent. The authors have found that the alerting services from hosting services such as HighWire are very useful. HighWire has operated a useful e-mail alerting service for some years. This informs librarians about the beginning and ending of free trial periods, and other relevant information such as activation dates. HighWire Press also sends around useful updates, for example, news of new publishers joining their free back issues program. (See <http://www.stanford.edu/dept/news/pr/01/highwire117.html>.) But HighWire has realized the need for further information regarding loss of access through a new subscription monitoring service. In an effort to assist ejournal administrators in libraries to avoid loss of access to online journals because of expired subscriptions, HighWire Press has created a service for administrators of ejournals "that will alert you when access from a particular subscription ends, and in some cases this service will allow you to get advance notice weeks in advance of loss of access" (Goodman). HighWire acknowledges that this won't solve all problems, but is a step in the right direction, particularly combined with the increasingly common publisher decision to allow a grace period for electronic access to journals around renewal time.

Ingenta has an alerting service called Ingenta announce <http://www. Ingenta.com/announce/index.html> but this does not appear regularly and the authors normally discover new Ingenta titles through publishers' and agents' alerting services, such as Swets Blackwell's Electronic Access Request Confirmation.

A useful publisher's alerting service is the newly established BMJ Journals Library Resource Centre, with its newsletter.

> Dear Subscription Administrator
> Re: BMJ Journals Library Resource Centre on www.bmjjournals. com
> This month sees the launch of the BMJ Journals Library Resource Centre (LRC). The LRC is a webpage designed specifically for librarians and subscription administrators. We would like to invite you to view the page at www.bmjjournals.com/subscriptions/ libraries.shtml. It contains information on pricing, site licenses, usage statistics, online journal features, FAQs and more. There is also a promotional resources section where you can download journal covers, logos, flyers and a poster (these can be downloaded for use on your intranet or in your own promotional pieces). The April 2003 newsletter can be found in the Newsletter/Updates section, it will be produced quarterly. To access the BMJ Journals Library Resource Centre please go to www.bmjjournals.com and click on the Library Resource Centre link. I do hope you find the webpage and newsletter useful. We are keen to have your feedback/comments so that we can make this a valuable resource for you (please use the feedback link on the website). (Halfacre)

We currently have a NESLI license to access almost all of the journals on Wiley InterScience. The other day I was visiting the Wiley site as part of routine maintenance to check whether issues were yet available for 2003 for a number of Wiley journals which had changed their title at the end of 2002, and which hadn't been online the last time I checked at the end of March 2003, plus a number of outstanding queries which hadn't yet been sorted. We all have these don't we. . . . I was pleasantly surprised, but also slightly miffed, to come across a new offering from Wiley InterScience, called the Discovery Newsletter, which provide information on journal title changes, cessations, etc. etc. http://www3.interscience.wiley.com/newsletter/index.html. What I was miffed about was why I hadn't been informed (as contact for the NESLI deal) about this newsletter, especially in view of the fact that I had recently been visited by a member of the Wiley marketing team, following on from my comments to this list about the splitting of some Wiley journals earlier in the year into separate parts. Several of my queries were sorted as a result of this meeting. But. . . . couldn't Wiley have alerted me to this new offering, or was I expected to find out about by accident? The newsletter is very helpful, but does contains some inaccuracies. If the publisher can't get this information correct, what chance have we? (Crawshaw 2003g)

Blackwell Publishers also provides a service which is less than helpful:

Dear Administrator
We have now updated your institutional account and administrator homepage with the following content:
Journal code: CCH, Cover year: 2003, Subscription type: Standard. . .
FromSynergy@blackwell-synergy.com

Similarly, Springer LINK provides two alerting services but there is no information on whether they are new titles; therefore, the ejournal administrators need to check the Alert list titles against current registered titles. Administrators also need to regular monitor registered titles as these often disappear from the subscription list or access is disabled.

Please note that the University of Melbourne LINK No. 1234567 (not our real number) previously maintained electronic access to

the titles contained in the Word attachment. They are also no longer appearing on our subscription list. Could you please urgently reinstate these titles or report upon their electronic status?
We also don't have a current subscription to the following titles on our subscription list, could you please remove these?
Dysphagia Springer title no. 00455
Supportive Care in Cancer Springer title no. 00520 (Crothers b)

While we are on the topic of communication how do other sites find messages from Springer Verlag telling you that some (unspecified) new titles are now accessible in LINK? How are we supposed to know which titles? I've been meaning to contact Springer to remind them it would be helpful if they could tell us which titles are new but since I seem to delete these messages on receipt I don't have any example to quote (and they may not know which message I'm referring to!) (Yamaguchi b)

Lesley Crawshaw also comments from her experience:

Re: Springer LINK Alert–if that is what you are referring to I would agree that it is pretty useless, just tells you more titles are available, but as Meiko has already said not which ones!! I know us librarians have got a reputation for being pretty good detectives, but that is going to[o] far! I do have an excerpt from one to back up Meiko's comments as to its unhelpfulness:

"Subject: More Titles accessible now in LINK

Your application for access to titles in LINK has been processed; The print subscription has been confirmed and access set up. Check the entire list of accessible titles at http://link.springer. de/cs/subli.htm

Any titles missing?"

As a more helpful alternative I would recommend the Springer LINK Serials Update which tells you which titles are new, which have ceased, which are no longer published by Springer etc. You can register for this at: http://link.springer.de/jour_update/index. htm. (Crawshaw 2003h)

Ejournal administrators need to consider whether it is beneficial to alert users while sorting out these problems, as this message from one of the public service staff at the University of Melbourne requested. "Is it possible to hide these titles while the subscription problem is being sorted out, or put a message in the remarks field about the subscription problems?" (Condron a).

CONCLUSION

This article provides an overview of ejournal life in a large academic library. It is relevant for other information service providers, particularly those colleagues working on the customer service side. The paper concentrates on problematic issues affecting information reference colleagues and those in liaison roles. It aims to increase their understanding of the many and varied access obstacles so that this knowledge assists them when encountering customer access problem queries.

REFERENCES

Abbott, Bruce. "Harcourt License for institutional online access." 20 March 2003, <reedelscustomers@lists.cc.utexas.edu> (20 March 2003).

Andrianopoulos, Alex. "Genetics Online." 14 February 2003, personal e-mail (14 February 2003).

Association of Subscription Agents. "ASA launches campaign on late pricing." 13 May 2002, <http://www.subscription-agents.org/pricing.html> (13 June 2003).

Baumle, Chris. "Journal of the American Dietetic Association." 14 March 2003, <reedelscustomers@lists.cc.utexas.edu> (14 March 2003).

Blackwell, Lisa. "Re: Publishers refusing to deal with a jobber (Dustin Larmore)." 22 May 2003, <SERIALST@LIST.UVM.EDU> (22 May 2003).

Bley, Robert. "E-Access Management and Much More" *Homepages: The Swets-Blackwell Magazine* 2 (2002): 4-5.

Cole, Louise (a). "A saga of subscription numbers." 14 April 2003, <LIS-E-JOURNALS@JISCMAIL.AC.UK> (14 April 2003).

_____ (b). "Ingenta and Ingenta select." 10 March 2003, <LIS-E-JOURNALS@JISCMAIL.AC.UK> (10 March 2003).

_____ (c). "Aslib problems continue for Leeds." 24 April 2003, <LIS-E-JOURNALS@JISCMAIL.AC.UK> (24 April 2003).

_____ (d). "American Medical Association titles." 10 March 2003, <LIS-E-JOURNALS@JISCMAIL.AC.UK> (10 March 2003).

_____ (e). "FW: new AGU subscription options announced (fwd)." 16 June 2003, <LIS-E-JOURNALS@JISCMAIL.AC.UK> (16 June 2003).

Condron, Patrick (a). "Re: Springer subscription list." 24 October 2002, personal e-mail (13 June 2003).

_____ (b). "CatchWord (Ingenta Select) vs Ingenta." 14 November 2002, personal e-mail (13 June 2003).

Conolly, Margaret. "RE: Anaesthesia and Intensive Care-online access." 11 April 2003, personal e-mail (11 April 2003).

Corbet Lauren. "Re: Elsevier position on Subscription Agents." 9 April 2003, <reedelscustomers@lists.cc.utexas.edu> (9 April 2003).

Crawshaw, Lesley (2002). "ACM Digital Library/IEEE Xplore-No Warning Given When Syntax of URLs Changed." 4 September 2002, <LIS-E-JOURNALS@JISCMAIL.AC.UK> (4 September 2002).

_____ (2003a). "Funny Things Happening on Ingenta Select with Taylor & Francis Journals." 1 Apr 2003, <LIS-E-JOURNALS@JISCMAIL.AC.UK> (1 April 2003).

_____ (2003b). "Statement from Aslib/Emerald re electronic journal access-a solution is on the horizon to the everchanging usernames and passwords." 1 May 2003, <LIS-E-JOURNALS@JISCMAIL.AC.UK> (1 May 2003).

_____ (2003c). "Grace Periods and Electronic Access to Journals." 3 January 2003, <LIS-E-JOURNALS@JISCMAIL.AC.UK> (3 January 2003).

_____ (2003d). "The Need for Better Feedback and Communication: American Journal of Sports Medicine: a Case Story." 11 April 2003, <LIS-E-JOURNALS@JISCMAIL.AC.UK> (11 April 2003).

_____ (2003e). "Re: American Medical Association titles." 10 March 2003, <LIS-E-JOURNALS@JISCMAIL.AC.UK> (10 March 2003).

_____ (2003f). "Did You Know Annual Reviews, Inc. Have Now Digitized Their Entire Backfile and Access is Available for a One-Time Payment." 4 June 2003, <LIS-E-JOURNALS@JISCMAIL.AC.UK> (4 June 2003).

_____ (2003g). "Wiley InterScience's New Discovery Newsletter-Couldn't They Have Informed Their Customers?" 23 May 2003, <LIS-E-JOURNALS@JISCMAIL.AC.UK> (23 May 2003).

_____ (2003h). "Re: Kluwer and Customer Service or Lack of It!" 29 January 2003, <LIS-E-JOURNALS@JISCMAIL.AC.UK> (29 January 2003).

Crothers, Stephen (a). "II account." 7 November 2002, personal e-mail (13 June 2003).

_____ (b). "Springer subscription list." 22 October 2002, personal e-mail (13 June 2003).

Dartnall, Jean. "Re: dealing directly with publishers–Linda Grooms." 14 March 2003, <SERIALST@LIST.UVM.EDU> (14 March 2003).

Davis, Phil. "Re: Journal of the American Dietetic Association." 14 March 2003, <reedelscustomers@lists.cc.utexas.edu> (14 March 2003).

Davis, Susan. "Re: Misleading statements on e-journal sites–Diane Paldan." 17 April 2003, <SERIALST@LIST.UVM.EDU> (17 April 2003).

Duraneceau, Ellen Finnie and Cindy Hepfer. "Staffing for electronic resource management: the results of a survey." *Serials Review* 28 (2002): 316-320.

Eastland, Barbara. "Re: Publishers refusing to deal with a jobber (Dustin Larmore)." 22 May 2003, <SERIALST@LIST.UVM.EDU> (22 May 2003).

French, Beverlee. "RE: Barriers to licensing e journals from some publishers." 28 May 2003, <http://www.cdlib.org/about/publications/licensingbarriers.html> (28 May 2003).

Funk, Mark. "AMA online journal pricing." 23 December 2002, <MEDLIB-L@ LISTSERV.BUFFALO.EDU> (13 June 2003).

Gacek, Elysia. "RE: Human Molecular Genetics-Electronic Customer no." 6 January 2003, personal e-mail (13 June 2003).

Goldstein, Cindy. "RE: Big Deals: one size does not fit all." 28 March 2003, <reedelscustomers@lists.cc.utexas.edu> (28 March 2003).

Goodman, David. "New subscription-monitoring service from Stanford's HighWire Press." 28 February 2003, <liblicense-1@lists.yale.edu> (28 February 2003).

Green, Toby. "FW: Grace Periods and Electronic Access to Journals." 6 January 2003, <LIS-E-JOURNALS@JISCMAIL.AC.UK> (6 January 2003).

Halfacre, Julie. "BMJ Library Resource Centre E-mail." 10 April 2003, distribution list (10 April 2003).

Hamaker, Chuck (a). "The New Elsevier's Surprising Service Problems." *The Charleston Advisor* 4 no. 3 (2003), <http://www.charlestonco.com/features.cfm?id=121&type=ed> (13 June 2003).

_____ (b). "More HHS institutional list with print." 28 March 2003, <reedelscustomers@ lists.cc.utexas.edu> (28 March 2003).

Harper, Paulina. "RE: Paraprofessional Staff working with e-journal procedures–Eleanor Cook." 6 March 2003, <SERIALST@LIST.UVM.EDU> (6 March 2003).

Hill, Claire (a). "RE: Ingenta Select access." 10 March 2003, personal e-mail (10 March 2003).

_____ (b). "RE: Ingenta Select access." 11 March 2003, personal e-mail (11 March 2003).

Hurcombe, Emma. "Re: a saga of subscription numbers." 14 April 2003, <LIS-E-JOURNALS@JISCMAIL.AC.UK> (14 April 2003).

Jasper, Richard. "RE: Librarians push back against complicated e-packages." 16 June 2003, <liblicense-1@lists.yale.edu> (16 June 2003).

Kaemper, Bernd-Christoph (a). "Perennial renewal problems with ASCE journals." 23 April 2003, <liblicense-1@lists.yale.edu> (23 April 2003).

_____ (b). "Perennial renewal problems with ASCE journals." 28 April 2003, <liblicense-1@ lists.yale.edu> (28 April 2003).

_____ (c). "Re: Harcourt journals on ScienceDirect." 20 March 2003, <reedelscustomers@ lists.cc.utexas.edu> (20 March 2003).

Kewley, Peter. "Subscription Agents: good or bad?" 11 March 2003, <LIS-LINK@ JISCMAIL.AC.UK> (11 March 2003).

King, Peter. "Re: Funny Things Happening on Ingenta Select with Taylor & Francis Journals." 1 April 2003, <LIS-E-JOURNALS@JISCMAIL.AC.UK> (1 April 2003).

Lewis, Nicholas. "Class B IP addresses not being accepted." 27 February 2003, <LIS-E-JOURNALS@JISCMAIL.AC.UK> (27 February 2003).

Martin, Deb. "PNAS Graces Institutional Subscriptions for 2003 (Vol 100)." 31 December 2002, <liblicense-1@lists.yale.edu> (13 June 2003).

Meddings, Kirsty. "IngentaSelect-some answers." 2 Apr 2003, <LIS-E-JOURNALS@ JISCMAIL.AC.UK> (2 April 2003).

Menefee, Daviess (a). "Elsevier position on Subscription Agents." 8 April 2003, <reedelscustomers@lists.cc.utexas.edu> (8 April 2003).

_____ (b). "Harcourt journals on ScienceDirect." 20 March 2003, <reedelscustomers@ lists.cc.utexas.edu> (20 March 2003).

Morris, Sally. "2002 Swets Blackwell E-journal Survey: Surveying the results." *Homepages: The Swets Blackwell Magazine* 2 (2002): 10-11.

Morris, Sandra. "Re: Taylor and Francis/Metapress." 14 March 2003, <LIS-E-JOURNALS@JISCMAIL.AC.UK> (14 March 2003).

Morse, Carol. "Re: Funny Things Happening on Ingenta Select with Taylor & Francis Journals." 1 April 2003, <LIS-E-JOURNALS@JISCMAIL.AC.UK> (1 April 2003).

Niles, Judith. "RE: Big Deals: one size does not fit all." 28 March 2003, <reedelscustomers@lists.cc.utexas.edu> (28 March 2003).

Noble, Richard. "Extended Gracing Period." 11 February 2003, <LIS-E-JOURNALS@JISCMAIL.AC.UK> (11 February 2003).

Norman, Frank. "Amer Soc Microbiol-no grace." 13 February 2003, <LIS-E-JOURNALS@JISCMAIL.AC.UK> (13 February 2003).

Orr, Christine. "2004 Prices for American Institute of Physics Archival Journals." 22 May 2003, <CHMINF-L@LISTSERV.INDIANA.EDU> (22 May 2003).

Oster, Dianne. "Re: Publishers refusing to deal with a jobber (Dustin Larmore)." 22 May 2003, <SERIALST@LIST.UVM.EDU> (22 May 2003).

Paldan, Diane. "Misleading statements on e-journal sites." 17 April 2003, <SERIALST@LIST.UVM.EDU> (17 April 2003).

Picerno, Peter. "RE: Librarians push back against complicated e-packages." 17 June 2003, <liblicense-l@lists.yale.edu> (17 June 2003).

Pinfield, Stephen. "Managing electronic library services: current issues in UK higher education institutions." *Ariadne* 29 (2001), <http://www.ariadne.ac.uk/issue29/pinfield/> (13 June 2003).

Pober, Stacy. "Ingenta journals on the web." 11 May 2003, <web4lib@sunsite.berkeley.edu> (11 May 2003).

Porter, George. "IEEE getting better at supporting libraries." 15 May 2003, <STS-L@LISTSERV.UTK.EDU> (15 May 2003).

Prabhu, Margaret. "Re: a saga of subscription numbers." 15 April 2003, <LIS-E-JOURNALS@JISCMAIL.AC.UK> (15 April 2003).

Roddham, Mike. "OUP pricing structure for online access." 12 March 2003, <LIS-MEDICAL@JISCMAIL.AC.UK> (12 March 2003).

Sinha, Rani. "Re: Perennial renewal problems with ASCE journals." 23 April 2003, <liblicense-l@lists.yale.edu> (23 April 2003).

Spada, M. "IEEE response to CalTech posting regarding IEEE library support." 16 May 2003, <SERIALST@LIST.UVM.EDU> (16 May 2003).

Stone, Graham. "Re: Funny Things Happening on Ingenta Select with Taylor & Francis Journals." 1 Apr 2003, <LIS-E-JOURNALS@JISCMAIL.AC.UK> (1 April 2003).

subscriptions@Catchword.com. "Online Access to Veterinary Anaesthesia and Analgesia."13 February 2003, personal e-mail (13 February 2003).

Synergy@blackwell-synergy.com. "Blackwell Synergy Account Updated." 18 March 2003, distribution list (18 March 2003).

Thompson, Ashleigh. "Re: Taylor and Francis/Metapress." 13 March 2003, <LIS-E-JOURNALS@JISCMAIL.AC.UK> (13 March 2003).

Troy, Anne. "British Jnl of Psychiatry sub." 4 February 2003, personal e-mail (4 February 2003).

Turner, Rollo. "Journal Administration-fragmentation or integration?" 7 November 2002, <http://www.subscription-agents.org/ejournaladmin.html> (13 June 2003).

Watkinson, Anthony. "Re: Oxford Journals Online Pricing Options 2004." 3 April 2003, <liblicense-l@lists.yale.edu> (3 April 2003).

Yamaguchi, Mieko (a). "Re: a saga of subscription numbers." 14 April 2003, <LIS-E-JOURNALS@JISCMAIL.AC.UK> (14 April 2003).

_____ (b). "Re: Kluwer and Customer Service or Lack of It!" 29 January 2003, <LIS-E-JOURNALS@JISCMAIL.AC.UK> (29 January 2003).

Electronic Reference Works
and Library Budgeting Dilemma

Ibironke O. Lawal

SUMMARY. The number of electronic resources has climbed up steadily in recent times. Some of these e-resources are reference sources, mostly in Science, Technology and Medicine (STM), which publishers convert to electronic for obvious reasons. The library budgets for materials usually have two main lines, budget for one time purchase (monographs) and budget for ongoing subscriptions (serials). It therefore becomes an issue when pricing model is not stable and this balance cannot be maintained. In understanding the importance of reference sources, this article examines the following: origin of reference service, information-seeking behavior of scientists and engineers, print versus online and user preference and expectations, nature accessibility and use of science reference texts, budgeting for and acquisitions of electronic science reference works. Do we have to adjust the budgets to accommodate the new trend or should publishers work within the framework of the library budgets? Some science librarians were interviewed and their responses were analyzed. Results revealed that: first, this is a common problem; second, most libraries still choose electronic over print irrespective; third, each institu-

Ibironke O. Lawal is Engineering and Science Librarian, James Branch Cabell Library, Virginia Commonwealth University, Richmond, VA 23284-2033 (E-mail: iolawal@vcu.edu).

[Haworth co-indexing entry note]: "Electronic Reference Works and Library Budgeting Dilemma." Lawal, Ibironke O. Co-published simultaneously in *The Acquisitions Librarian* (The Haworth Information Press, an imprint of The Haworth Press, Inc.) Vol. 19, No. 1/2 (#37/38), 2007, pp. 47-62; and: *Collection Development Issues in the Online Environment* (ed: Di Su) The Haworth Information Press, an imprint of The Haworth Press, Inc., 2007, pp. 47-62. Single or multiple copies of this article are available for a fee from The Haworth Document Delivery Service [1-800-HAWORTH, 9:00 a.m. - 5:00 p.m. (EST). E-mail address: docdelivery@haworthpress.com].

doi:10.1300/J101v19n37_04

tion deals with the problem on a case by case basis; fourth, most libraries have no permanent solutions yet. *[Article copies available for a fee from The Haworth Document Delivery Service: 1-800-HAWORTH. E-mail address: <docdelivery@haworthpress.com> Website: <http://www.HaworthPress.com> © 2007 by The Haworth Press, Inc. All rights reserved.]*

KEYWORDS. Acquisitions, budgeting, electronic resources, information-seeking behavior, pricing model, reference texts, reference work, science reference works

INTRODUCTION

Over the past few centuries, general library service in academic libraries has undergone significant transformations. Clienteles of the first academic libraries did not enjoy free access to books. The rules ordered in 1667 by the Harvard Overseers stipulated that no undergraduate in the college shall borrow a book out of the library, and further, that no graduate (unless it be a fellow) shall borrow a book without the permission of the President (Massachusetts 1925). (But by 1765, Harvard students had borrowing privileges (Brough 1949).) The Yale Trustees voted a rule with similar provisions in 1723 (Dexter 1916). In the early nineteenth century, the Libraries of Oxford and Cambridge still had books in chains (Clark 1901). At Columbia, in 1844, the library opened for only two and a half hours, three days a week (Jewett 1850). In 1849 during the term time, the Yale College Library was open five hours daily except Sundays and Holidays (Jewett 1850 p. 71). Throughout the colonial period, books in libraries were few and precious and the authorities placed a higher premium on their safekeeping than on making them immediately useful. The libraries had no necessary bearing on the studies of the undergraduates (Brough 1949).

A special committee appointed in 1866 by the Harvard Board of Governors stated, that the usefulness of books largely depends upon the facility of access and convenience attending them and that a building which is merely a place for their deposit and safe keeping has no claim to be called a library (University 1867). Today, patrons not only have access to library resources for longer hours (some libraries open 24 hours, seven days a week), they can borrow books for a considerable period of time.

ORIGIN OF REFERENCE WORK

Librarians, in their effort to make books increasingly useful, paid more attention to the reader. Hence the concept of reference service in American Libraries originated as aid to readers. William Child defined reference work as:

> assistance given by a librarian to readers in acquainting them with the intricacies of the catalog in answering questions and in short, doing anything and everything in his power to facilitate access to resources of the library in his charge. (Child 1891)

Other definitions include those of Alice Kroeger (Kroeger 1902) and William Warner Bishop (Bishop 1915). Margaret Hutchins of Columbia School of Library Service defined reference work as that which

> includes direct personal aid within a library to persons in search of information for whatever purpose and also various library activities especially aimed at making information as easily available as possible. Selecting and organizing material with this end in view is as important a part of reference work as their interpretation to the individual reader. (Hutchins 1944)

But my favorite definition is that given by Lucy Edwards:

> Reference work is not only, as the phrase suggests, the use of books on the premises, as against borrowing them for home reading, but an individual and a personal service to each reader, to enable him to obtain the information he requires with the greatest ease, and the least possible delay. (Edwards 1951)

These definitions do not say anything about reference books or reference rooms, implying that these are not indispensable for reference work.

Some librarians had the overarching notion that helping readers would be a distraction from the librarian's important duties and therefore, as many reference books as possible should be made easily available in reading rooms so that the time of the librarian and assistants might be spent on other duties (Rothstein 1989). For colleges, at this time, libraries were meagerly supported, opened for only a few hours and with less trained personnel, the library was still very much at the periphery. The custodial function was more important. The student who could not borrow a book from the library had little or no demands for personal assistance; hence development of reference service was slow. The first proposal of a program of personal assistance to readers was by Samuel Green in a paper delivered at the 1876 librarians' conference. Green stated that the more a librarian mingles with readers and the greater the amount of assistance he renders to them, the more intense does the conviction of the citizens, also become that the library is a useful institution. They will then be more willing to grant money in larger and sums to be used in buying books and employing additional staff (Green 1876). His motive was to increase use of the collection in the 'Green Library,' a collection of scholarly books given with the stipulation that they were to be used only within the library. By encouraging readers to come up with questions, which might draw upon the resources he was able to show a distinct statistical increase in the use of the library. College librarians gradually adopted Green's position. A librarian should be much more than a keeper of books; he should be an educator. It was only when the college library would change from a sacred ground to "workshop" that reference service could be made possible and for this change, it was the new ideas in teaching that were primarily responsible. This new direction saw the library as laboratory for professors and students. This view focussed the attention of librarians upon the needs of their clientele and led them to look for new means of meeting those needs. The library, therefore offers the best bibliographies, cyclopedias, dictionaries and other works of reference. Organized reference work as a library service did not gain recognition until the third quarter of the nineteenth century. Neither the proceedings of the Librarians' Conference of 1853, nor the *Report on Public Libraries in the United States* of 1876 (which represented the next generation of American Librarianship), treated the issue of helping readers seriously. The concept of reference service thus born in the later part of the 1800s has evolved and 'assistance to readers' persists till today.

INFORMATION-SEEKING BEHAVIOR

Librarians of today, make efforts to enable the reader to obtain all the information desired with ease and with minimum amount of delay. As the library service evolved, so did the information-seeking behavior and expectations of readers. In the decades prior to the 1990s, students use print indexes and abstracts and other print sources for their course work and for research. Loretta Caren and Arleen Somerville noted that in the 1980s, print sources were easy to use because online sources needed searching intermediary or extensive training (Caren 1986). In Pelzer's study, of information-seeking behavior of veterinary medicine students at Iowa State University in 1988, the only computerized index used by more than 5% of the students was Veterinary Bulletin, which had been used by 12% of the sophomores and 22% of the juniors. Use decreased 4% and 8% in the freshmen and senior classes (Pelzer 1988). In the early years of 1990s CD-ROM was the newest innovation that was causing changes in reference departments, and in many libraries, stand-alone CD-ROM databases were the first digital resources used by library patrons without intermediary assistance (with the exception of the library catalog). By the middle of the decade, CD-ROM was well established and more often networked and the first end-user online services (led by OCLC's FirstSearch) appeared, empowering users to search for online information and formulate online searches independent of librarian's assistance (Kyrillidou 2000). This trend began to lure users away from the printed periodical indexes that for decades had been the mainstay of many research trips to the library. The 1990s were a decade of phenomenal technological advancements in the library world and of profound change in the way library users went about seeking information. It was the decade that the Internet became widely available and the World Wide Web a convenient medium. The book as a printed entity now has the rivalry of digital resources, which became immediately popular among users. As progress is made in the digital arena, publishers and producers of information began to manufacture their products specifically with end-users in mind, and to market them directly to users. In this way, users are able to access the information without the intervention of the librarian. Few at the time had heard of anything called the World Wide Web, and access to full-text resources, except perhaps through a vendor produced database such as Lexis-Nexis or Dialog. With the onset of the World Wide Web, began a whole new way of delivering information. It slowly gained grounds in popularity. The use style of clientele changed over the years. Users today have become more technologically advanced and are able to search, explore and discover on their own. But as electronic resources proliferate, some scientists become overwhelmed with information explosion and keeping current in their various fields, so much so that they revert to relying on librarians for their information needs. According to Julie Bichteler and Dederick Ward, dependence of library users on librarians increases as geologists have less and less time for information seeking (Bichteler 1989).

The survey done by Tenopir and Ennis, revealed that expectation of both reference staff members and patrons changed profoundly during the last decade of the century as well. Now both groups believe that an answer to almost every question can be found if the right combination of resources and search strategies is chosen from the multitude of Web resources and online services accessible (Tenopir 2002). Access to good secondary sources with as much full text as possible is clearly important to meet these heightened expectations.

Such is the flexibility, immediacy, and ubiquity of electronic resources that libraries began to see the decline of reference transactions. According to Association of Research Libraries (ARL) statistics of eighty three ARL Libraries, average annual percentage change from 1991-1999 was 0.3% (Kyrillidou 2000). Studies show that users tend to choose the easier, more convenient, method that requires less time and the least amount of effort. Hence, they prefer electronic access because of ease of access, self-served mode, and new ways of using information which could not be done with the print, such as incorporation of texts and images directly into manuscripts. The nature of academic reference work has changed in the last decade. Changes are taking place but what do they mean for the libraries? More sources and format options, higher patron expectations more reliance on new technologies create a dynamic environment. Libraries have to move fast but can their budgets keep up with the fast pace of technology?

PRINT versus ELECTRONIC

Advantages of electronic resources have been documented in recent literature. Ginsparg, Neal, Harnard, Bachrach, and Lawal all have eminently stated the various benefits of electronic over print resources (Lawal 2002). Due to these advantages, users prefer the electronic to print and have new forms of expectations from libraries. In a study of veterinary medical students, Pelzer, Wiese, and Leysen found that although basic uses of the library remained unchanged after ten years, information seeking had shifted toward the Internet and use of electronic resources during that time. Almost 60% of the students reported using the Internet for locating current information and most of them indicated that electronic resources would have some degree of importance to them for future education needs (Pelzer 1998). A survey of health sciences faculty information-seeking methods at the University of Illinois at Chicago documented behavior in transition from print to electronic resources and also established the preferred location for information access as the office (Curtis 1997). Cecilia Brown, in her study at University of Oklahoma shows that scientists are embracing electronic bibliographic databases and would like to see the access to and the capabilities of these expanded (Brown 1999). Carlson reports that at the University of Idaho, the number of electronic articles that Idaho students retrieved went up about 350 percent and periodical database searches shot up by almost 800 percent (Carlson 2001).

These findings point to the fact that users prefer the electronic resources to print. The primary goal of science libraries should be then, to obtain access to as many appropriate electronic reference sources and finding aids as possible. STM reference sources fall into different categories according to (Voigt Melvin 1961).

NATURE AND USE OF SCIENCE REFERENCE TEXTS

For scientists, Voigt recognized three approaches to information. First, is the need to keep up to date with current progress of a scientist's field called, the 'current approach.' Second, is the need that comes to the scientist in the course of his work—a need for some specific information essential to his experimental work or an understanding of that work. This need for a bit of data, a method, the construction of a piece of apparatus, an equation, an explanation of an observed phenomenon, a definition, comes to a researcher regularly in his work. This is called the 'everyday approach.' Third, is the need to check through all of the relevant information, existing on a given topic usually the specific one that the researcher is working on. The need arises when a researcher starts work on a new investigation or when he is writing up the results for publication, a lecture, or a patent application. This is called the 'exhaustive approach' (Voigt 1961). This paper is mostly about the sources used in the second approach. Most of the information wanted in this 'everyday approach' is specific. It could be physical data, a method of analysis or synthesis, information concerning an apparatus, its construction or use, a mathematical formula, derivation, equation, a table, a description of a substance, an organism, an interpretation of certain phenomena, or spectra information. Though conversation with colleagues top the list of resources used, many still rely on published information. In Biological sciences for instance, handbooks and books of methods (*Methods in*

Enzymology) in general and lists and checklists in case of systematics in particular. In engineering, in Kremer's study, handbooks are considered most important followed by standards and specifications (Kremer 1980). Example of handbooks in Engineering is *Engnetbase*, a CRC database of 135 engineering handbooks. In medicine, *MD Consult* has over 40 reference books and patient education materials. In chemistry, the 'everyday approach' assumes greater importance because most areas of chemistry are closely tied to the literature. General reference works used most for everyday approach include encyclopedias, treatises, handbooks, and monographs. The encyclopedias most often used are the comprehensive ones covering large areas such as *Kirk Othmer's Encyclopedia of Chemical Technology* and *Ullmanns Encyclopedia of Industrial Chemistry*. Volumes of tables and data are equally important. *CRC Handbook of Chemistry and Physics*, *Perry's Chemical Engineers Handbook*, and *Lange's Handbook of Chemistry* are used for common data. In the publisher's words, *Lange's Handbook of Chemistry* is a reference volume for all requiring ready access to chemical and physical data used in laboratory work and manufacturing.

   Ullmann's Encyclopedia of Industrial Chemistry constitutes a significant source of numerical and factual data, which obviously must remain current if it is to be useful. Information in Ullmann's is browsed, read, and absorbed, and so, not well adapted to the standard techniques of traditional on-line data access. At the same time, revisions released in the form of printed supplements do not serve the encyclopedia well. Preparing a completely new set of Ullmanns, requires a great deal of time and a massive amount of commitments. By the time a new edition is completed, the earlier volumes will already be seriously out of date. The solution is to convert the data to an interactive Ullmann's presenting all the print data but enhancing it to be consistent with an electronic product (Russey 1995). The publisher of Ullmann's therefore produced a CD-ROM of the entire work. At regular intervals–probably annually, and at relatively modest cost, the entire work will be replaced on a subscription basis by a new disk. The new disk will offer a substantially revised data base, with more recent production figures, the latest insights into current and projected industrial practices and trends, and new versions of key articles deemed to be either weak or obsolete (Russey 1995). Ullmanns is now a Web-based product with an annual subscription. The same applies to *Kirk-Othmer's Encyclopedia of Chemical Technology*, which is also now, a Web-based product with an annual license, but the option to buy only the print is still available. (See Table 1.)

TABLE 1. Selected Reference Sources That Used to Be Print Only, but Now Have Electronic Versions

Title	Comments	Electronic Version
Access Perry	Site License, combines Perry's Chemical Engineers Handbook, 7th ed, Chemical Properties handbook, 1st edition, and Lange's Handbook of Chemistry, 15th edition	2000+
CRC Handbook of Physics and Chemistry	Site license	83rd edition,
Chemnetbase	Includes Combined Chemical Dictionaries (CCD), offered only as a site license	1999+
Combined Chemical Dictionary	Chapman and Hall nine major reference works in chemical information, now included in Chemnetbase	2001+
Encyclopedia Britannica	New, combined with Webster Dictionary and Britannica Book of the Year. Offers both institutional and personal license on an annual basis	1994+
Encyclopedia of Electrical and Electronics Engineering	Licensed on an annual basis	1999+
Encyclopedia of Immunology, 2nd edition	Licensed on an annual basis	1999+
Engnetbase	135 CRC handbooks in Engineering and allied sciences	2000+
Kirk Othmer's Encyclopedia of Chemical Technology	Licensed on an annual basis, with an option to purchase content and a subscription for annual updates	2000+
Lange's Handbook of Chemistry	Included in Knovel, also in Access Perry	15th edition, 1999
Merck Index	Personal and institutional annual subscriptions	13th edition
MD Consult	Over 40 medical reference books included. Licensed on an annual basis	1997+
Perry's Chemical Engineers Handbook	Included in Knovel, also in Access Perry	7th edition, 1997
Properties of Organic Compounds	Now included in Chemnetbase	1999+ Version 6. CD-ROM 2000
Ullmanns Encyclopedia of Industrial Chemistry, 6th edition	Licensed on an annual basis, only the contents, no archival option	First on Networkable CD-ROM, then on the Web in 1997+

The publisher in these two examples changed the format to suite the nature of the product doing what they think is valuable for the user, but without the thought of the rigid library budgetary structure. Obviously, there are a number of advantages to converting to electronic. Apart from the currency of the content, they offer simultaneous multiple user access, complex search regimens and the possibility of downloading relevant entries to a local workstation, to be examined later at one's own convenience. Other materials in this approach are *Standards*. In the past, many libraries bought *Standards* on a just-in-case basis. But as funding became scarce, and format changed from print to electronic, many libraries changed the acquisitions of *Standards* to on-demand model. Predictability of costs is a basic tenet of budget preparation. Unpredictable costs associated with on-demand purchases are very difficult to manage in academic budgets. Several scholars have written about budgeting and electronic resources. Both Leyden and Johnston stated how difficult it is to contain the new format within the existing budgetary limits of the library. According to Johnston:

> The significant and rapid rise of electronic resources in what one might term the electronic anti-collection, and the way in which collection development librarians are attempting to balance local holdings versus access, are representative of a major change from the old, stable access/ownership paradigm to a new one which is far from stable. (Johnston 1996)

Lynden, of Brown University, noted that his institution could not continue to purchase electronic materials without shifting costs from print materials, an action that has political bearings (Lynden 1999). Though writings on budgeting and electronic resources abound in the literature, none has addressed the issue of reference works as a separate entity. There has been a proliferation of electronic reference works in STM, which require leasing contracts as opposed to one time payment as it is done with print. Judging from the way that budget is projected and allocated in most libraries, the shift in format creates a budgeting dilemma.

LIBRARY FUNDING

Most of the budgetary problems libraries have are due to poor funding. This is not a recent issue. Poor funding in libraries had existed since the nineteenth century. In 1870, the Commissioner of Education reported a total of 369 colleges in the United States (Education 1870). Many of these institutions were small and struggling for bare survival and, could not be reasonably expected to develop libraries, which would equal those of older colleges. Scanty funds constituted one limitation. The cultural resources of the states varied tremendously then, as they do now and consequently, public colleges had little opportunity to build their collections through the accumulation of gifts. Older institutions in addition to the obvious advantage afforded by their longer period of existence had larger numbers of loyal alumni whom they could depend for support (Brough 1949).

Of thirteen librarians interviewed, only one stated his institution converts to electronic version as soon as available. One stated that they do retain both and eleven stated they do not convert immediately. All eleven attributed their decisions to budgetary reasons. Five say they do not have money to subscribe. One librarian says that they make the decision not to buy a particular e-resource because cost per use is too high or the quality of the product may not worth the cost. When asked what they do if they have to purchase the electronic, five say they shift money from monographs to fund the new resource. According to Martha Kyrillidou, ARL statistics show that during the last decade, libraries shifted expenditures from monographs to serials to meet some of the demands of increasing serial prices, reducing the number of monographs purchased by 26% (Kyrillidou 2000).

> Monograph expenditures although rising somewhat steadily in recent years have been increasing at a much slower pace to accommodate the ever-increasing serial expenditures and new electronic resources. (Kyrillidou 2000)

In spite of this, libraries continue to add electronic reference works to their collection. More than half of the librarians interviewed said they still add reference e-resources. One librarian says that online sources are more likely to be used than print because they are available anytime, anywhere. Re-allocation of funds allows them to provide better service to their patrons. When asked how they pay for these, one librarian says they pay through their consortium. Another one says if serials are cancelled or cease publication, they divert that money to fund the new format, but if the print reference tool is only available in electronic format, there will be funds available for it. One says they have to cancel the print though the money does not usually match up. One librarian says the electronic has to compete with other materials for the limited funds. Similarly, another one says overall material budget is used, which impacts print collection. In another library, any new resource, regardless of format is funded from the monographic funds, though there is an option of applying for some special funding. On the other side of the coin, one librarian says they are dropping electronic access to some e-encyclopedias and buying paper version because the electronic is harder to use.

Fueled by lack of funding and full-text technology, some libraries establish an on-demand purchasing for materials such as *Standards*. This means a certain amount of money is allocated for purchase as requests by clientele are made. This on-demand funding creates a new problem because it is hard to predict demand and cost. Prices of *Standards* vary widely from one end to the other and all in between.

ELECTRONIC REFERENCE AND BUDGETING

Although budgeting issues have been a topic of discussion in the literature for several decades, shifting from one time payment to a subscription is a relatively new phenomenon not yet found in current literature. How can libraries resolve this emerging trend? Frederick Lynden listed three requirements for budgets, namely:

- they should be an estimate, often itemized, of expected income and expense;
- they should be a plan of operation based upon an estimate;
- they should serve as an estimate of funds for a given period.

Electronic materials defy these requirements because they have such a variety of payment options that it is hard to estimate expense. Furthermore, they are published without much advance notice and so decrease funds for other formats (Lynden 1999). Lynden also identified three issues that emanate from publishers, namely, accessibility issues–paper with electronic or electronic only; access issues–location, number of simultaneous users or number of passwords, additional charges for printing or downloading; networked or stand alone; consortia issues–prices vary according to size and negotiation ability of the consortium. Other issues include product characteristics such as overlap of titles. For instance, some publishers or aggregators combine related reference sources into a single database which they lease to libraries. Examples of these are *CRC Handbook of Chemistry and Physics* and *Properties of Organic Compounds* sold separately but also included in Chemnetbase; Knovel which is an aggregation of 502 top scientific and engineering references, including Sax's *Dangerous Properties of Industrial Materials*, 10th edition (3 volumes), and *Sittigs Handbook of Toxic and Hazardous Chemicals and Carcinogens*, 4th edition (Table 1). Prices are not stable because each library or consortium negotiates its own price and pledges not to disclose. How can publishers help? Current mode of payment for the electronic reference sources that change format is mostly unsatisfactory. The practice of diverting money from monographic funds to pay for an unexpected electronic reference cannot go on indefinitely. The following suggestions might help to address the problem.

For publishers:

1. It is the same information, why do we have to pay for it every year? Charge small amounts for updates periodically.
2. Make the electronic one time purchases as well. One librarian states that her institution has been working very hard to get publishers to think about how they create the pricing models for their electronic book products (especially vendors of handbook types of materials), encouraging them to create models based on a one-time fee for content and a smaller ongoing maintenance fee. (I believe publishers are beginning to understand libraries' budgetary structure. They now offer one time purchase options which also allow libraries to own the archives.)
3. Give adequate advance notice in anticipation of a resource going electronic, to enable librarians scout for funds.
4. Give a period of grace when the resource would be free.
5. Be flexible in payment options (i.e., allow installments–some publishers are already doing this).

For librarians:

1. Have a definite electronic policy that governs e-reference sources. (Only 4 out of 13 librarians interviewed have electronic collection policies.)
2. Have some emergency funds available, and at the end of the year, if not spent, can be used for journal prepayment.

It is easier to theorize than to put into action. Some might say that these suggestions are not doable steps in the direction of resolving the issue, but we have to start somewhere.

CONCLUSION

Martha Kyrillidou says, as the research library environment moves to even speedier networks with the development of Internet2 and Next Generation Initiative (NGI), issues related to mechanisms for establishing access and costs for managing content on such networks are fundamental concerns for the library of the future. I cannot agree with her more. Libraries have a long way to go. Users' needs and expectations have evolved with increasing technological advancements. Today's library patrons particularly the Millennials (seventeen year olds) do not consider the Internet as new technology. It is something taken for granted. They have zero tolerance for delays; there is a strong demand for immediacy. The library today has a lot of competition and has to deliver if it wants to stay competitive and remain in business. So far, many libraries are holding up under the pressure, but still have to cross many hurdles, as far as budgetary issues are concerned. Pricing for electronic resources is still unstable. It is still evolving and librarians are finding the transition problematic. Libraries are noted for making necessary adjustments in order to continue to provide excellent service to their clientele. It is time to revise library budgetary practices in line with the current electronic market to provide a lasting solution. But do librarians have to do all the adjustments? It is necessary for publishers and vendors to implement pricing strategies that will work for all stakeholders. It is only in the spirit of cooperation that we all can win.

REFERENCES

Bichteler, Julie and Dederick Ward. 1989. Information-seeking behavior of geoscientists. *Special Libraries* 80 (Summer): 169-178.

Bishop, William Warner. 1915. The theory of reference work. *Bulletin of the American Library Association* IX: 134-139.

Brough, James. 1949. Evolving conceptions of library service in four American universities: Chicago, Columbia, Harvard, Yale, 1876-1946. Dissertation, School of Education, Stanford University, Stanford, California.

Brown, Cecilia M. 1999. Information seeking behavior of scientists in the electronic information age: Astronomers, chemists, mathematicians and physicists. *Journal of the American Society for Information Science* 50 (10): 929-943.

Caren, Loretta and Arleen Somerville. 1986. Online versus print sources in academic scientific and technical libraries: Supplement or replacement? *Science & Technology Libraries* 6 (4): 45-59.

Carlson, S. 2001. The deserted library. *The Chronicle of Higher Education* XLVII (12): A35-A38.

Child, William B. 1891. Reference work at the Columbia College Library. *Library Journal* XVI (October): 298.

Clark, John Willis. 1901. *The Care of Books*. Cambridge: University Press.

Curtis, Karen L., Ann C. Weller and Julie M. Hurd. 1997. Information-seeking behavior of health sciences faculty: The impact of new information technologies. *Bulletin of the Medical Library Association* 85 (4): 402-410.

Dexter, Franklin Bowditch (eds.). 1916. *Documentary History of Yale University Under the Original Charter of the Collegiate School of Connecticut, 1701-1745*. New Haven: Yale University Press.

Education, US Bureau of. 1870. *Report of the Commission of Education*. Washington, D.C.: Government Printing Office.

Edwards, Lucy I. 1951. Reference work in municipal libraries. In *The Reference Librarian in University, Municipal and Specialised Libraries*, edited by J. D. Stewart. London: Grafton.

Green, Samuel Swett. 1876. Personal relations between librarians and readers. *Library Journal* I (October): 74-81.

Hutchins, Margaret. 1944. *Introduction to Reference Work*. Chicago: American Library Association.

Jewett, Charles Coffin. 1850. *Appendix to the Report of the Board of Regents of the Smithsonian Institution, Containing a Report on the Public Libraries of the United States of America, January 1, 1850, 31st Congress, 1st Session, Senate Miscellaneous Documents No. 120*. Washington: Printed for the Senate.

Johnston, B. J. and Victoria Witte. 1996. Electronic resources and budgeting: Funding at the edge. *Collection Management* 21 (1): 3-16.

Kremer, Jeannette M. 1980. Information flow among engineers in a design company. Dissertation, University of Illinois, Urbana-Champaign.

Kroeger, Alice Bertha. 1902. *Guide to the Study and Use of Reference Books: A Manual for Librarians*. Boston and New York: Houghton Mifflin Co.

Kyrillidou, Martha. 2000. Research library trends: ARL statistics. *Journal of Academic Librarianship* 26: 427-436.

Lawal, Ibironke O. 2002. Science resources: Does the Internet make them cheaper, better? *Bottom Line: Managing Library Finances* 15 (3): 116-124.

Lynden, F. C. 1999. Budgeting for collection development in the electronic environment. *Journal of Library Administration* 28 (4): 37-56.

Massachusetts, Colonial Society of. 1925. *Publications*. Vol. XV, *Harvard College Records Parts I and III*. Boston: Harvard.

Pelzer, Nancy L. and Joan M. Leysen. 1988. Library use and information-seeking behavior of veterinary medical students. *Bulletin of the Medical Library Association* 76 (4): 328-333.

Pelzer, Nancy L., William H. Wiese and Joan M. Leysen. 1998. Library use and information seeking behavior of veterinary medical students revisited in the electronic environment. *Bulletin of the Medical Library Association* 86 (3): 346-355.

Rothstein, Samuel. 1989. The development of the concept of reference service in American libraries, 1850-1900. [Reprinted from *Libr Q Ja* '53.] *The Reference Librarian* no. 25-26: 7-31.

Russey, William E. 1995. Reference works in science: Revolutionary evolution. *Collection Management* 19 (3/4): 125-130.

Tenopir, Carol and Lisa Ennis. 2002. A decade of digital reference 1991-2001. *Reference & User Services Quarterly* 41 (3): 264-273.

University, Harvard. 1867. *Proceedings of the Board of Overseers of Harvard College Library, 1863-1867.* Boston: Press of Geo C. Rand and Avery.

Voigt, Melvin J. 1961. *Scientist' approaches to information.* Edited by R. E. Stevens. *ACRL Monograph 24*: American Library Association.

Going E-Only:
A Feasible Option
in the Current UK Journals Marketplace?

Martin Wolf

SUMMARY. Provides a case study of the acquisitions processes that were necessary when Cardiff University's School of Engineering made a decision to subscribe to electronic-only versions of journals where such subscriptions were less expensive than the print equivalent. In doing so, addresses issues of electronic subscriptions management in UK academic institutions such as national initiatives, subscription models, and the impact of tax regulations. Also describes some new developments in the scholarly communication marketplace. Concludes that the current ejournal marketplace is not conducive to moving to electronic-only journal subscriptions as a cost-saving measure, but new developments may in the near future fundamentally alter the journals marketplace. *[Article copies available for a fee from The Haworth Document Delivery Service: 1-800-HAWORTH. E-mail address: <docdelivery@haworthpress.com> Website: <http://www.HaworthPress.com> © 2007 by The Haworth Press, Inc. All rights reserved.]*

Martin Wolf is Social Sciences Librarian, University of Warwick Library, Gibbet Hill Road, Coventry, CV4 7AL, United Kingdom (E-mail: M.Wolf@warwick.ac.uk).

The author gratefully acknowledges the assistance of Kathryn Hudson in the preparation of parts of this paper.

[Haworth co-indexing entry note]: "Going E-Only: A Feasible Option in the Current UK Journals Marketplace?" Wolf, Martin. Co-published simultaneously in *The Acquisitions Librarian* (The Haworth Information Press, an imprint of The Haworth Press, Inc.) Vol. 19, No. 1/2 (#37/38), 2007, pp. 63-74; and: *Collection Development Issues in the Online Environment* (ed: Di Su) The Haworth Information Press, an imprint of The Haworth Press, Inc., 2007, pp. 63-74. Single or multiple copies of this article are available for a fee from The Haworth Document Delivery Service [1-800-HAWORTH, 9:00 a.m. - 5:00 p.m. (EST). E-mail address: docdelivery@haworthpress.com].

doi:10.1300/J101v19n37_05

KEYWORDS. Academic libraries, Cardiff University, electronic journals, Europe, journals management, serials management, tax, United Kingdom, universities

INTRODUCTION

This article examines what was necessary when the School of Engineering at Cardiff University in the UK made a decision to pursue electronic-only versions of its journal subscriptions. Cardiff University is one of the most successful research universities in the UK, ranking 7th in the 2001 Research Assessment Exercise.[1] The Information Services division (INFOS) provides an integrated library and computing support service to the university. In examining the acquisitions processes of locating and subscribing to electronic-only versions of engineering journals the article provides a brief overview of ejournal developments in the UK, a case study of how the INFOS acquisitions department dealt with this challenge (highlighting some of the major issues of ejournals management), and some pointers to possible future developments.

FUNDING OF EJOURNALS AT CARDIFF UNIVERSITY

Like many UK universities, Cardiff University operates with a devolved budgeting structure. This means that most monies for the acquisition of library and information resources are under the control of individual academic departments. Subject information specialists liaise with departments over the purchase of information resources, recommending new resources as appropriate, but final decisions on purchasing resources rest with individual departments.

A separate Reference & Information fund is held by INFOS. Originally used solely for the purchase of key reference materials, this fund is now also used for subscriptions to large, multi-disciplinary resources in those cases where difficulties might be encountered in securing equitable contributions from a range of different academic departments; examples of such resources include Elsevier's ScienceDirect ejournals service and the ISI's Web of Knowledge databases. The development of multi-disciplinary ejournal packages has placed an increasing burden on the Reference & Information fund, and suggests a need for a redistribution of funds so that more funding is under the direct control of INFOS. This may be addressed in the near future as Cardiff University prepares to merge with the University of Wales College of Medicine, an institution where control of serials budgets rests with library staff, rather than academic staff.

Particular challenges can be faced when publishers offer bundled print and electronic subscription packages for their titles. In the devolved budget structure, print journal subscriptions are wholly funded by the subscribing department, but electronic subscriptions are sometimes funded with a mixture of departmental and Reference & Information funds. A Reference & Information group, comprising staff from across INFOS (including acquisitions and cataloguing staff, information specialists, and IT support staff) meets regularly to discuss new information resources. This forum has proved extremely useful in ensuring that funding for new information resources such as ejournals has been found, despite the difficulties sometimes encountered in securing departmental consortia funding for resources. It has been successful in driving policy on electronic information resources, and actively engages in promotional work to highlight the usefulness of ejournals and other resources by "pump priming" from central funds information resources that academic departments might wish to fund in later years.

ACQUISITIONS PROCEDURES

Cardiff University has a serials ordering system in which internal order forms must be physically signed by departmental signatories to authorises payment from that department's fund for information resources. Purchase orders are generated using the Voyager library management system and then sent to the subscription agents Swets Blackwell. As part of the Southern Universities Purchasing Consortium (SUPC) the university receives discounts on its journal subscriptions. Although most subscriptions are via the agents Swets Blackwell, a large number of titles from smaller and more specialised publishers (such as publishers of legal material) are dealt with on an individual basis. As ejournals increasingly become the standard format for journal delivery, a slight trend towards dealing directly with publishers, rather than through subscription agents, can be detected.

NESLI AND UK EJOURNALS POLICY

No study of the ejournals marketplace in UK academia can be complete without mention of NESLI[2] (the National Electronic Site License

Initiative). NESLI was established in 1998 by the Joint Information Systems Committee[3] (JISC), a national body funded by all UK post-16 and higher education funding councils to provide guidance in, and promotion of, the use of information technology to support learning, research and administration in education. Intended to run until 2001, NESLI was extended until 2002, and has now been replaced by NESLi2.

NESLI promoted the take up of ejournals within UK academia by negotiating with publishers on behalf of the higher education community. NESLI negotiations focused on obtaining value-for-money ejournal subscriptions from leading publishers, as well as dealing with matters such as access (for example, by providing a website through which all NESLI-negotiated ejournal subscriptions could be accessed) and authentication. It also created the Model Site Licence,[4] which all providers of ejournals were encouraged to use. This licence has helped to provide a modicum of stability in a marketplace crowded with diverse, competing subscription models. Cardiff University has taken up NESLI-negotiated offers since the project's inception, and seeks to subscribe to ejournals which conform as closely as possible to the terms of the model licence.

USAGE OF EJOURNALS AT CARDIFF UNIVERSITY

The Cardiff University community has access to ejournals through a range of access points. The most important of these is the Voyager OPAC. The catalogue contains combined print and electronic records, i.e., print holdings and links to electronic versions of journals are presented on the same results screen. Though Internet links were originally part of the 856 MARC holdings field, it is intended to move to having internet links in the bibliographic record upon subscription to the SerialsSolutions[5] ejournal management service. Access to ejournals is also provided via an in-house database (to be replaced by SerialsSolutions), and through static links on web pages of subject-based resources maintained by subject information specialists.

INFOS is committed to open communication with its customers in order to provide the best possible service, and to this end engages in regular consultation with the university community. A web-based survey of academics in three selected departments indicated there was a strong preference amongst staff for using ejournals rather than print.[6] This preference was based almost solely on the desktop access afforded by ejournals, and did not indicate a belief that ejournals are qualitatively better than their print equivalents.

A later consultation with all departments, conducted by subject information specialists, confirmed that this view was true for all departments. It also confirmed that most academics do not feel it is yet possible to cancel print subscriptions wholesale in favour of electronic-only subscription models. Departments are reluctant to give up their print subscriptions as they consider print journals important both for long-term access to content and for the serendipitous discovery of information that can arise from browsing the pages of print journals. In this regard, then, the School of Engineering is unique amongst the university's departments in being prepared to take electronic-only subscriptions as its favoured choice.

THE DECISION TO GO E-ONLY

The School of Engineering (ENGIN) based its decision to subscribe to electronic-only journals largely on budgetary issues. The school felt that by taking electronic-only subscriptions, as opposed to bundled print and electronic offers, they could realise savings in their information resources budget. In this they differed from other examples of institutions making a decision to pursue electronic-only journal subscriptions as a qualitative measure, such as Drexel University, which "in 1998 . . . made migration to an electronic journal collection as quickly as possible a key component of its [library's] strategic plan."[7]

This had a direct impact on acquisitions staff's efforts to fulfil the department's wish. Not only did they have to establish those titles to which ENGIN subscribes that were available in electronic-only format, but then check those subscription options to see if they were cheaper than a print or bundled print and electronic subscription. This was one of the main challenges faced during the process of going e-only for ENGIN.

GOING E-ONLY: THE ACQUISITIONS PROCESSES

The following notes describe how INFOS acquisitions staff attempted to fulfil the brief of finding cheaper electronic-only subscription options for the School of Engineering's journal titles. In doing so they highlight some of the current issues in the UK ejournals marketplace.

The biggest challenge facing acquisition staff was the sheer range of different subscription models on offer. With few standards yet to emerge in the ejournal marketplace, despite initiatives such as NESLI, it was necessary for staff to check a multitude of different options to see if it was in fact possible to subscribe to an electronic-only version of a journal, and if doing so would result in cost savings. The subscription agents Swets Blackwell were asked to provide a list of those titles available electronically funded by ENGIN. This list was then checked in-house to investigate price differences between the various subscription options available.

As indicated earlier not all subscriptions are taken via Swets Blackwell, and in the case of these subscriptions acquisitions staff had to make direct contact with publishers to investigate the possibility of subscribing only to the electronic version of titles. This was a time-intensive process, exacerbated by the timing of ENGIN's request to pursue electronic-only subscriptions where doing so would yield cost savings. The request was received in August 2001, and journal renewals were due to be finished at the end of September. Time constraints were therefore another factor in attempting to fulfil the brief from ENGIN.

Some of the subscription models offered to UK universities include:

- Models where electronic access to a title is "free" with subscription to the print version (where the price of the print version may have in fact risen by as much as 20%);
- Models where access to electronic versions of all a publisher's output is priced according to current expenditure on that publisher's print journals, with the need to agree to "no print cancellations" policies;
- Models where a "current subscription" gives access to the previous five years' worth of content, and a separate subscription is required for material older than five years–such a model leading to institutions having to pay twice for the same content.

The bewildering array of different subscription models can make the task of migrating from print to electronic-only journal subscriptions difficult. In the specific case of ENGIN's subscriptions one obstacle encountered in attempting to migrate to less expensive electronic-only subscriptions was the fact that in many cases access to the electronic version of titles was explicitly linked to the relevant print subscription.

Some publishers place severe restrictions on the number of print subscriptions that can be cancelled when moving to electronic access. Where print cancellations are technically available, doing so will often eliminate the right to discounts on the electronic versions. This leads to a belief that the "big deals" such as ScienceDirect are here to stay, as publishers can see that by tying their electronic subscription models to print subscriptions they can both protect their present income streams from print journals and create additional revenue by charging for electronic access to those titles.

Perhaps ironically, then, it was one such large publisher deal that provided one of the main successes in the attempt to migrate to cheaper electronic-only versions of ENGIN subscriptions, in the shape of the IEEEXplore service from the Institute of Electrical and Electronics Engineers, Inc. This service provides full text access to IEEE transactions, journals, magazines and conference proceedings, and provided the opportunity to cancel all print subscriptions to IEEE publications. This in itself created much additional work in the short term, as, although a single invoice was received for the IEEEXplore service, print subscriptions had to be cancelled on the library's internal acquisitions module on an individual title-by-title basis.

IEEEXplore proved the exception to the rule, however, as in many other cases it was impossible to meet ENGIN's requirements of finding electronic-only subscriptions options that were less expensive than print or print with electronic subscriptions. If an academic department were to take the decision to move to electronic-only subscriptions as a qualitative measure, rather than a budget measure, the process of migrating to electronic-only subscriptions would be more straightforward, as it was discovered during the process that many journals are available in electronic-only format at the same or higher price than the relevant print title. However, in this case study it was found that the current marketplace is not offering cheaper electronic versions of print journals.

Possibly the main contributory factor to the expense of electronic journals in the UK is the imposition of VAT (Value Added Tax) on electronic journal subscriptions. The current full UK rate of VAT is 17.5%. Under European Union law, VAT is charged on "electronic services," and this category of service includes electronic journals. In the case of bundled print and electronic journal subscription models difficulties can be encountered in determining on what amount of the total subscription cost VAT should be imposed, though this is largely a matter for the suppliers themselves, rather than libraries. In the case of electronic-only subscriptions, however, it is clear that VAT is due on the whole of the subscription cost. So, while it was possible to locate electronic-only versions of engineering journals that had the same base price as the printed version, the imposition of the 17.5% VAT rate would make the electronic-only subscription more expensive.

During the time frame being described there was also a great deal of uncertainty over the status of VAT on electronic journals from non-EU suppliers, who do not charge VAT. The university could be held liable by the UK treasury to pay VAT on these products, but the situation was unclear as the VAT would need to be calculated by the university, not the supplier, and as mentioned above, establishing the proportion of a bundled subscription cost on which VAT is payable can be very difficult.

Despite the efforts of campaign groups such as the Frankfurt Group and the Digital Content Forum[8] (whose members include the Association of Learned and Professional Society Publishers[9] and The Publishers Association[10]) to win an exemption from the full VAT rate for electronic publications, the EU Directive on VAT and e-commerce that came into effect on 1st July 2003 makes the payment of VAT on electronic journals compulsory, as the requirement to pay VAT is now dependant on the country in which the services are received, rather than the country from which they are supplied. This means that when subscribing to electronic journals from non-EU suppliers, the university is responsible for accounting for UK VAT using reverse charge mechanisms. As such, the extra costs incurred by VAT limited acquisitions staffs' ability to locate less-expensive electronic-only versions of ENGIN's journal subscriptions.

MANAGING THE PROCESS

The process of pursuing electronic-only subscriptions for ENGIN did not only impact the work of the acquisitions team; other parts of INFOS were involved as well. Work for cataloguers included closing holdings for cancelled print titles and setting up links to the electronic versions, while information specialists had to update their static lists of links to ejournals. The amount of administrative effort required for the successful management of electronic journals is one of the major challenges facing library services as they provide access to increasing numbers of electronic titles. INFOS staff, faced with a plurality of access routes to journal content, now spend more time than ever before in contact with suppliers, particularly when access to a title is disrupted for

any reason, as discovering what exactly has gone wrong, and then recti-
fying that problem, can take a considerable time (Turner provides a
good summary of these issues from the subscription agent's perspective[11]). Such work can include dealing with proxy access, negotiating licenses (a growing concern in the light of Cardiff University's upcoming
merger with the University of Wales College of Medicine, which has library sites throughout Wales), arranging passwords, ensuring that journal URLs are kept up-to-date, etc.

INFOS is well-equipped to deal with these challenges. Alongside acquisitions staff we have a dedicated Electronic Journals Co-ordinator
managing access to titles on a day-by-day basis, and a specific Information Resources Support team who are responsible for ensuring compliance with licenses. The department has also recently (August 2003)
subscribed to the SerialsSolutions electronic journals management system, which should reduce staff time spent on aspects of electronic journals management such as maintaining MARC records in the Voyager
catalogue and ensuring continuity of access to titles held in aggregator
databases.

FUTURE DEVELOPMENTS

While it is clear that ejournals and other electronic information resources will become increasingly important aspects of library service portfolios, it is not clear what forms those resources might take.
Certainly the proliferation of different subscription models from the
commercial publishers shows no sign of abating, creating extra administrative work for those involved in resource acquisition. However,
new developments in journal publishing models may soon acquire
enough critical mass to alter fundamentally the journals marketplace.

Ejournal publishers are now beginning to be more flexible in their
provision of unbundled subscription options (i.e., those that do not
"force" subscribers to take both print and electronic formats). The UK
government's Office of Fair Trading warned in September 2002[12] that it
was concerned at journal price increases far above the rate of inflation,
the substantial price differences between commercial and non-commer-
cial journals, and the possibility that the bundling of print and ejournals
by large publishers could prevent smaller publishers entering the marketplace. Their report concluded that if competition within the sector
failed to improve they would consider if further action, possibly conducted internationally, would be necessary.

There are developments and initiatives within the ejournals market-place seeking to create that degree of competition. SPARC[13] (Scholarly Publications and Academic Resources Coalition) brings together research libraries, universities and other organisations interested in what it sees as the "crisis" in scholarly communication.[14] Part of this involves promoting competitively-priced journals (called SPARC Alternatives) that are direct equivalents of established, more-expensive titles. Similarly, the Public Library of Science, a non-profit organisation of scientists seeking to make the scientific, technical and medical literature a freely available public resource, is seeking to use the internet to provide "immediate unrestricted access to scientific ideas, methods, results, and conclusions [to] speed the progress of science and medicine."[15] Its first step is the launch in October 2003 of *PloS Biology*, a freely-accessible, peer-reviewed journal.

As part of its remit to promote the use of new technology in the support of research and learning in the UK, the JISC has recently funded membership of BioMed Central for all UK higher education institutions. BioMed Central publish a range of journals that can be either freely-accessible to all, freely accessible to registered users, or available to subscribers, the publication of which is funded by charging contributors an article-processing fee. By funding BioMed Central membership for all UK higher education institutions, the JISC has created the opportunity for UK academics to submit their articles to BioMed Central journals without incurring any fees themselves. All research articles accepted by BioMed Central are also immediately deposited with at least one open access repository, such as PubMed Central.

Open access repositories (also known as open access archives) are repositories of pre- and post-publication papers (eprints) and other digital content that are catalogued with standard, open archive-compliant metadata.[16] Such repositories can be institution-based[17] (e.g., Dspace from Massachusetts Institute of Technology[18]) or subject-based (e.g., the famous Los Alamos Preprint server for physics and related disciplines, now known as arXiv[19] and hosted by Cornell University). By using standard open archives metadata, the records in such repositories can be searched and accessed by a range of services known as Open Access Metadata Harvesters.[20] These services allow the simultaneous cross-searching of many open access repositories, giving users the opportunity to find information from a very wide range of sources. As services like these grow in number and academic acceptance, it is possible that increasing numbers of journal readers will search for individual papers available electronically, rather than using journals as we currently know them. INFOS has been active in promoting such services to the Cardiff University academic community, and is following developments with interest.

SUMMARY

This article has provided a brief case study on the issues raised by trying to provide electronic-only journal subscriptions to the engineering department of a large, research-led UK university, where such subscriptions would be less expensive than print or print and electronic options. In doing so it has drawn attention to some of the key issues within the current ejournals marketplace, including the proliferation of subscription models and the cost issues involved in the application of Value Added Tax to electronic services. Taken in conjunction with the national ejournals initiatives mentioned, these indicate that the current ejournal marketplace is not conducive to moving to electronic-only journals subscriptions as a cost-saving measure. New developments and alternatives to traditional journal publishing, however, indicate that major changes in the provision of scholarly information may soon affect the whole ejournals acquisitions process.

REFERENCES

All URLs checked and working on 22 August 2003.

1. Cardiff University, "Research quality-RAE Results" (2001) available at: <http://www.cf.ac.uk/news/research_quality/>.
2. NESLi2, <http://www.nesli2.ac.uk>.
3. JISC–The Join Information Systems Committee, <http://www.jisc.ac.uk>.
4. NESLI model licence, <http://www.nesli2.ac.uk/model.htm>.
5. For more information, see the SerialsSolutions website at: <http://www.serialssolutions.com>.
6. Martin Wolf "Electronic journals-use, evaluation and policy," *Information Services and Use* 21 (3/4) (2001):249-261.
7. Carol Hansen Montgomery "Measuring the impact of an electronic journal collection on library costs: A framework and preliminary observations," Dlib 6 (10) (2000) available at: <http://www.dlib.org/dlib/october00/montgomery/10montgomery.html>.
8. Digital Content Forum, <http://www.dcf.org.uk>.
9. Association of Learned and Professional Society Publishers, <http://www.alpsp.org>.
10. The Publishers Association, <http://www.publishers.org.uk>.

11. Rollo Turner, "Ejournal administration-fragmentation or integration?" (2002) available at: <http://www.subscription-agents.org/ejournaladmin.html>.

12. Office of Fair Trading "Can the scientific journals market work better?" (2002) available at: <http://www.oft.gov.uk/News/Press+releases/2002/PN+55-02+Can+the+scientific+journals+market+work+better.htm>.

13. SPARC, <http://www.arl.org/sparc>.

14. For a fuller description of the history and future direction of SPARC, see: Mary Case, "Igniting change in scholarly communication: SPARC, its past, present and future," *Advances in librarianship* 26 (2002):1-28 Also available at: <http://www.arl.org/sparc/SPARC_Advances.pdf>.

15. Public Library of Science, <http://www.publiclibraryofscience.org>.

16. For more information, see the Open Archives initiative at: <http://www.openarchives.org>.

17. For a description of institutional eprint archives, see: Raym Crow, "The case for institutional repositories: a SPARC position paper," (2002), available at: <http://www.arl.org/sparc/IR/IR_Final_Release_102.pdf>.

18. Dspace, <http://libraries.mit.edu/dspace>.

19. arXiv, <http://arxiv.org>.

20. For an example of an Open Archives Metadata Harvesters, see: OAIster <http://oaister.umdl.umich.edu/o/oaister/>.

Are Electronic Serials Helping or Hindering Academic Libraries?

Leila I. T. Wallenius

SUMMARY. As academic libraries move toward the electronic frontier for their serial subscriptions, there are several issues to be considered. This paper intends to outline the advantages and disadvantages with respect to electronic and paper serials, address selection criteria, and describe our practice in coping with these issues at the Leddy Library of the University of Windsor, Canada. *[Article copies available for a fee from The Haworth Document Delivery Service: 1-800-HAWORTH. E-mail address: <docdelivery@haworthpress.com> Website: <http://www.HaworthPress.com> © 2007 by The Haworth Press, Inc. All rights reserved.]*

KEYWORDS. Canada, electronic serials, Leddy Library, Ontario, print serials, University of Windsor, virtual reference service

INTRODUCTION

Universities and colleges throughout the world are moving toward a focus on electronic serial publications. As libraries purchase more and more electronic-only serials and make decisions to switch from print to

---

Leila I. T. Wallenius is Head of Reference, Leddy Library, University of Windsor, Windsor, ON N9B 3P4, Canada (E-mail: leilaw@uwindsor.ca).

[Haworth co-indexing entry note]: "Are Electronic Serials Helping or Hindering Academic Libraries?" Wallenius, Leila I. T. Co-published simultaneously in *The Acquisitions Librarian* (The Haworth Information Press, an imprint of The Haworth Press, Inc.) Vol. 19, No. 1/2 (#37/38), 2007, pp. 75-82; and: *Collection Development Issues in the Online Environment* (ed: Di Su) The Haworth Information Press, an imprint of The Haworth Press, Inc., 2007, pp. 75-82. Single or multiple copies of this article are available for a fee from The Haworth Document Delivery Service [1-800-HAWORTH, 9:00 a.m. - 5:00 p.m. (EST). E-mail address: docdelivery@haworthpress.com].

Available online at http://www.haworthpress.com/web/AL
© 2007 by The Haworth Press, Inc. All rights reserved.
doi:10.1300/J101v19n37_06

electronic, there are several issues to be considered regarding the acquisition and maintenance of serials.

The physical space within libraries has been constantly problematic. The shelves are full, and libraries are attempting to find ways of making room in their buildings for new materials. One common solution is to use off-site storage for materials that are rarely used or weed unnecessary collections to make room for the new materials. As libraries move to electronic subscriptions to replace the print serials, they are liberating physical space for new title acquisitions. Decisions need to be made on whether or not to keep the back files in paper if the items are now owned electronically. In Ontario, the university libraries are seriously considering the necessity of having one or two paper copies of electronically available journals.

PRINT SERIALS:
ISSUES TO CONSIDER

The availability of the electronic serials has had a major effect on acquisitions and serial maintenance of print serials. What are some of the implications of these changes in subscription format? What does it mean for our physical handling of the serial materials? Are there other implications that academic libraries have not considered?

For years we have been dealing with many issues surrounding the receipt of paper journals. First of all, and probably the most important, is the challenge of claiming. Issues that are not received have always been a problem. To identify a missing item requires personnel to continually verify the status of paper subscriptions. Often times, a missing issue was caught only when the next issue has arrived. As automation has come to serials processing, libraries have been better able to track the expected delivery dates of issues and thereby prepare for claiming in advance.

Even with these improvements in libraries' claiming processes, many publishers are changing their operation patterns that challenge libraries' ability to manage their print serial collections. For example, some publishers have moved to shorter print runs for their serial titles. As a result, libraries must ensure that claiming occurs in a timely manner. If claims are not processed quickly enough, the possibility of not getting an expected issue increases. Issues that are not received result in gaps in holdings. Another example, some publishers are moving to electronic storage of serial runs, and thus being able to offer print-on-demand service. As print-on-demand becomes more popular, libraries may be able to have fewer missing issues, but will need to create and integrate the print-on-demand type of claim into their operations.

The physical receipt of journals has always been a time consuming process. There has been progress made in this area through the use of smart barcode technology for journal issues. Libraries hope that in the not so distant future they will spend less time manually processing print serial issues, and thus liberate staff time for other professional activities.

In some libraries second copies have been purchased solely for the purpose of ensuring that there will be a complete run of a particular journal for binding. Buying second copies for binding obviously adds to the amount of money libraries spend on print serial subscriptions. Since budget dollars are always hard to come by, it would be preferable to allow this second copy money to be used for other purposes, such as paying for additional electronic fee or new acquisitions.

For most libraries binding print serials has always meant that for a few weeks a year, or even longer, the most recent volume or volumes of a journal would be unavailable to the library's community. Materials would be pulled from shelves, processed and shipped to the commercial binder. Even with quick binding the material would be missing for at least a few days. While factoring in the cost of staff time in the journal binding process, it is the physical binding that appears to be one of the most time intensive aspects of print serials maintenance.

ELECTRONIC SERIALS: ISSUES TO CONSIDER

The advantages of electronic serials are numerous. One of the principle reasons for many of us moving to electronic is that it gives libraries the ability to offer faculty and students significantly enhanced serial collections. Another beneficial aspect is that electronic resources allow libraries to expend their collections continually without adding the physical bulk in their buildings. This is especially important, as the renewal of library buildings is not necessarily keeping up with demand.

One of the main advantages of electronic subscription is that the materials are available 24/7.[1] Also, the electronic version is available well before the print journal arrives in the library. Furthermore, electronic materials are never signed out. They are, in theory, always available whenever a patron wants to look at a particular article or journal. There is no need to bind nor do the issues go missing.

The use of electronic journals is never as simple as one would hope. Many have experienced the problem of going to a journal site and finding that, for whatever reason, the item you are looking for is not actually there. Rupp-Serrano et al. suggest it may be important to maintain a print copy in the collection particularly if the journal is essential. On the other hand, they also point out that many accrediting organizations are finally moving away from the principle that print is prim mentality.[2]

Geleijnse, in 1997, listed several benefits when KUB moved toward electronic access for their Elsevier journals:

1. The information would always be available, 24 hours a day; the journal would never be at the bindery, stolen, or unavailable; and
2. Important management information for collection development would be gathered on the real use of journals.[3]

It is the expectation of always having access to everything that causes a potential problem. It is difficult to explain to our users why the item they are looking for is not available, especially when most of the journal is there online. Geleijnse suggests that "libraries will have to make [the issue] about whether to subscribe to journals, to have campus-wide licenses on electronic files of these journals, or to rely on interlibrary loan, document delivery, or pay-per view agreements with publishers or intermediaries."[4]

At the Leddy Library of the University of Windsor, interlibrary loan and document delivery are used to supplement electronic and paper serial subscriptions. Faculty and graduate students may request interlibrary loan and document delivery basically free of charge. Undergraduates, however, must pay a fee for these services. Undergraduates, therefore, may find it difficult to get the journal articles they need if those articles are not in the University of Windsor's local collections. To solve this problem, Leddy Library made a concerted effort to increase or at least maintain subscriptions to journals that support early undergraduate research. As a result, our 1st year students may be able to find most of the materials that they need in the library's local collections, while the 4th year students, doing more in-depth research, may utilize the library's interlibrary loan and document delivery services to supplement and enhance their research resources.

In Canada and beyond, many libraries and researchers use the Canadian Institute for Scientific and Technical Information (CISTI) and CISTI Source to delivery their scientific and technical literature. This is a service whose time has come. Their document delivery service is of excellent quality, and turnaround time is prompt even during the peak periods of the year.

The decision of whether or not to keep both print and electronic subscriptions should always depend upon the situation in the particular library. For the complete journal suites from major publishers such as Elsevier, Wiley, and Kluwer, these issues are more straightforward than those of aggregated databases such as ProQuest or Wilson. In a brief e-mail survey of Ontario universities, the majority indicated that they would cancel print copy of a journal subscription if they had reliable access to the electronic copy of the journal. Two institutions indicated that they were also canceling subscriptions of certain print titles since the titles were also available in the aggregator databases that they subscribe. This is a far cry from where these universities were five years ago when most institutions were very cautiously entering the world of electronic serials and often maintaining print copies of titles in addition to the electronic.

In the case of aggregated databases the issues may be complicated. The decision to cancel print titles for the aggregator version may be simple if the journal is completely reproduced in the online version. However, aggregators do not necessarily provide complete cover-to-cover reproduction of journal issues, nor are issues added to the aggregator's database always in a timely manner. The most significant problem with aggregator databases is that there can be substantial embargos on the release of the electronic copy from the publisher. Depending on the length of the embargo period and the individual libraries' criteria for selecting or deselecting journal titles, the library may have to decide whether it should carry both paper copy and the aggregated electronic version. In Ontario it is interesting to note that there are only two institutions that are canceling print subscriptions to the journals that are part of aggregator databases. The only situation that these two institutions would probably keep the paper copy is when there is a substantial embargo period, or some visual content of the journal is not reproduced or not effectively reproduced in the electronic version.

Another significant issue with a third party aggregator is the maintenance of holdings for the library. Most providers send out notifications of changes in electronic holdings. It is then up to the library to make the necessary changes to the holdings statements. This is usually not a problem when a new title is added to the database. It is more difficult to deal with when an electronic subscription is cancelled or a title disappears from the aggregator database. The library may need to review the situation and decide whether or not to re-subscribe to the journal, either in paper or in electronic format from another database source. These changes in a library's access to electronic serials can prove to be critical if funding is tight and the library cannot afford re-subscribe to the journal in paper. Depending on how critical the title is to the library, it may trigger a collection development issue since the interruption in subscription may create unwanted gaps in the library's holdings. These gaps in holdings are the issues that must always be considered.

It may appear that the addition of new titles to aggregator files or the deletion of other titles is not a major staffing issue. However, there is still a need to maintain the integrity of library online catalogues. Furthermore, if the library has determined that there should be no duplication of print with electronic, how does the library manage the process of print cancellations, the switch to electronic only, and the possibility of having to re-subscribe to journal titles as their availability changes? Libraries often need to consider budgetary impacts, such as cancellations of print titles that overlap with electronic subscription, dealing with monitoring refunds from print titles, tracking changing subscription periods between print and electronic, and making decisions on whether to pursue electronic subscriptions through vendors or directly from publishers.

As far as budget is concerned, bundled deals could be a consideration because bundled packages through aggregators, such as Wilson Omnifile, ABI-Inform, and EBSCO, offer substantial savings over purchasing all the individual full-text titles.

The reality of our electronic collections is that materials may not be owed but rather rented or leased, and "that the individual title content is not selected by the library."[5] Librarians should become educated consumers of full-text databases, particularly if they are considering substituting electronic versions for print subscriptions.

Some libraries are cataloguing their electronic resources and at the same time maintaining lists of e-resources on their Web pages. Does this duplication of effort make sense in the modern environment? According to Kalyan, there is a need as we move toward the electronic frontier to have better homepage access and access to the curriculum, and library instruction to promote information literacy skills among users of the electronic resources.[6] In fact, many libraries are attempting to provide this better homepage access while maintaining their OPACs in order to provide the most effective access for their patrons.

OTHER ISSUES:
THE ROLE OF REFERENCE SERVICES

There are many issues about the advantages or disadvantages of electronic journals. How do these changes in our serial subscriptions affect the research of our faculty and students? Carol Tenopir implies that the academic pursuits of the students and faculty may be changing with electronic publishing. In her paper of 2003 she states that "it is difficult to make sure that students know how to select appropriate resources, evaluate the quality of what they select, and use these resources well regardless of format or medium."[7] Tenopir may be correct in her estimation that our role in helping students is reduced in this new environment. Our perceptions of how important librarians are to student research may have been overestimated. Reference statistics indicate that most libraries are interacting with a very small proportion of their student population on a daily basis at the reference desk. Also, our interactions with these students can vary greatly. Asking where a specific collection is located is significantly different from asking about how to evaluate specific resources for their research.

It is our duty to guide students to appropriate resources for their research in today's digital environment. Many librarians have found that students are using the Web to do much of their research, but not necessarily being able to distinguish between the scholarly resources provided by the library and materials that are freely available on the Web that may be of questionable veracity and value. This is an important issue which should be addressed in our teaching of library skills.

On a bright side, virtual reference has grown in use among academic libraries. The usage of Leddy Library's virtual reference services indicates that there is clearly a need for the students working remotely to have access to assistance from the library. Since Leddy's virtual reference service was implemented more than two years ago, the demand for this service has more than tripled. Leddy Library expects that the demand for virtual reference services will continue to grow, and is therefore looking for ways to integrate the virtual reference service more completely into standard reference services.

CONCLUSION

There are no easy answers to many of the issues involved with the balance between print and electronic serial publications. Being aware of these issues provides some help to libraries operating in this new digital environment. As libraries strive for the goal of providing 24/7 access to as much material as possible, it is important to consider and evaluate these issues in order to enhance the collections of the library and provide better access and services for the client. There will be a continuing need to augment services such as virtual reference service. It should be the role of the library to provide not only these materials whenever and wherever they are needed, but also the expertise and assistance in how to use these resources effectively.

REFERENCES

1. Kalyan, Sulekha. "Non-renewal of print journal subscriptions that duplicate titles in selected electronic databases: A case study." *Library Collections Acquisitions, & Technical Services*, vol 26, 2002, pp. 409-421.

2. Rupp-Serrano, Karen, Sarah Robbins and Danielle Cain. "Canceling print serials in favor of electronic: Criteria for decision making." *Library Collections Acquisitions, & Technical Services*, vol 26, 2002, pp. 369-378.

3. Geleijnse, Hans. "The KUB's experience with electronic subscriptions." *Library Acquisitions: Practice & Theory*, vol. 21, no. 3, 1997, pp. 297-302.

4. Ibid.

5. Kalyan.

6. Kalyan.

7. Tenopir, Carol. "Electronic publishing: Research issues for academic librarians and users." *Library Trends*, vol 51, no 4, Spring 2003, pp. 614-635.

SPECIAL ISSUES

DMCA, CTEA, UCITA . . . Oh My!
An Overview of Copyright Law and Its Impact on Library Acquisitions and Collection Development of Electronic Resources

Leslie A. Lee
Michelle M. Wu

SUMMARY. The purpose of traditional copyright law was to encourage the creation of works based on and to ensure reasonable access to original thought. Despite this harmonious intent, an intrinsic tension exists between libraries and copyright holders, as the former promotes

Leslie A. Lee is Assistant Director for Administration, George Washington University, Jacob Burns Law Library, 716 20th Street NW, Washington, DC 20052 (E-mail: llee@law.gwu.edu). Michelle M. Wu is Director of the Deane Law Library/Associate Professor of Law, Hofstra University School of Law, 121 Hofstra University, Hempstead, NY 11549 (E-mail: lawmmw@hofstra.edu).

[Haworth co-indexing entry note]: "DMCA, CTEA, UCITA . . . Oh My! An Overview of Copyright Law and Its Impact on Library Acquisitions and Collection Development of Electronic Resources." Lee, Leslie A., and Michelle M. Wu. Co-published simultaneously in *The Acquisitions Librarian* (The Haworth Information Press, an imprint of The Haworth Press, Inc.) Vol. 19, No. 1/2 (#37/38), 2007, pp. 83-97; and: *Collection Development Issues in the Online Environment* (ed: Di Su) The Haworth Information Press, an imprint of The Haworth Press, Inc., 2007, pp. 83-97. Single or multiple copies of this article are available for a fee from The Haworth Document Delivery Service [1-800-HAWORTH, 9:00 a.m. - 5:00 p.m. (EST). E-mail address: docdelivery@haworthpress.com].

doi:10.1300/J101v19n37_07

"free" access to information that ultimately reduces the income of the latter. The expansion of copyright laws to electronic documents has shifted the balance between these two interests. This article discusses recent copyright legislation and case law as well as provides an overview of the practical effects of these laws on day-to-day library acquisitions, collection development, and collection management activities. *[Article copies available for a fee from The Haworth Document Delivery Service: 1-800-HAWORTH. E-mail address: <docdelivery@haworthpress.com> Website: <http://www.HaworthPress.com> © 2007 by The Haworth Press, Inc. All rights reserved.]*

KEYWORDS. Acquisitions, case law, collection development, collection management, copyright, electronic documents, legislation, libraries

INTRODUCTION

Whether we realize it or not, we are in fact bumping up against copyright questions on a daily basis. If we do not manage them to our advantage, they will manage us and dictate how we conduct our scholarly work.[1]

Copyright is a fact of life for libraries, not only for the more commonly known, practical reasons, such as photocopying print resources or acquiring and making accessible electronic subscriptions, but also for a more philosophical one–that libraries represent a compromise in the law's intent to balance the competing rights of the author against those of the public. The purpose of traditional copyright law was to encourage the creation of works based on and to ensure reasonable access to original thought. Theoretically, the author would reap rewards during a limited period of time, after which he would be motivated to develop new ideas to generate income, and the public would have unfettered use of the "old" knowledge on which to build a more advanced and sophisticated future. Existing copyright laws reflect such an intent by providing access to the public through a number of exceptions pertinent to libraries, including fair use, performances and displays in classrooms or distance learning, backup copies of software applications, and creation of formats for persons with disabilities.[2]

Despite this harmonious intent, an intrinsic tension exists between libraries and copyright holders, as the former promotes "free" access to information that ultimately reduces the income of the latter.[3] The expansion of copyright laws to electronic documents has shifted the balance between these two interests. Copyright, which is already governed by a complex interpretation of laws, has become increasingly difficult to understand in its application to electronic materials, in large part because it has not kept pace with technological advances. The governing laws either persist in confining electronic documents to the print world or they fail to consider the inherent flexibility of technology.

Further complicating the analysis, many of the rules governing copyright–such as the concept of fair use–have been developed outside of enacted legislation. While the four prongs relevant in a fair use determination eventually were codified in section 107 of the *United States Code*, the legislature deliberately drafted ambiguous language[4] so as to accommodate future technologies. This same vagueness has infected subsequent pieces of legislation, compelling users to rely on expensive and unwieldy court decisions to provide substance where Congress left gaps.

This article will discuss recent copyright legislation and case law as well as provide an overview of the practical effects of these laws on day-to-day library acquisitions, collection development and collection management activities. The target audience is academic libraries, though aspects of this article may apply to other types of libraries.

Please be advised that due to the rapid change of copyright law and technology, some facts will most likely be out-of-date at the time of publication. Readers should note that the research for this article is current through late 2002/early 2003; for the prevailing law, please consult the appropriate legislative and judicial sources.

LEGISLATION

The impact of copyright legislation on libraries has not always been directly or immediately apparent. Although library organizations such as the American Library Association (ALA) and the American Association of Law Libraries (AALL) have been vocal in supporting or opposing proposed copyright legislation, libraries are usually not the primary focus of such laws. Nonetheless, libraries frequently are adversely affected by these laws, and must lobby vigorously to retain their rights through imperfect exemptions. A summary of key legislation follows:

Digital Millennium Copyright Act[5]

The Digital Millennium Copyright Act, hereinafter DMCA, a sweeping set of laws enacted in October 1998, changed the concept of fair use as it applies to electronic documents. It did so by expanding permissible technological controls over activities formerly governed only by law and by individual compliance with the law. Although the act provides exemptions for libraries and archives, such as expressly permitting digitization of works in fragile condition and allowing libraries to create digital reproductions of works stored in obsolete formats, each exception has strict stipulations.

Known as anti-circumvention provisions, the DMCA's technological restrictions on access, reproduction, and distribution, in particular, have affected libraries and their ability to make fair use of materials. Since the technological controls placed on electronic resources are limited only by dexterity and imagination, publishers can thwart fair use of these resources by using electronic display-only manacles on the documents. In other words, unless a user wants to transcribe an article by hand, constraints on the ability to print a news article can effectively impede a user's ability to distribute it, even if the distribution would have been legal under fair use.

Further, some of the act's anti-circumvention provisions have "created a whole new level of protection for digital works that was previously unavailable under copyright law, essentially banning the tools of copying rather than banning copying itself."[6] Decryption, characterized as a technological means to regulate access to a work, is expressly prohibited.[7] The use of digital data, which requires machine intervention to be read, inherently involves decryption. As such, prohibiting decryption results in complete copyright holder control over the piece. Should a library want to archive materials, it would be unable to regain access to them legally. Should users want to download a portion of an article, they may likewise be violating DMCA provisions.

As mentioned in the beginning of this section, the DMCA did incorporate some exceptions for libraries. One such provision, section 103(d), which amends title 17, section 1201(d) of the *United States Code*, permits nonprofit libraries, archives, and educational institutions limited rights to decrypt security controls if they are reviewing a work in good faith consideration of purchasing it. However, the rights are very restrictive, terminating immediately at the conclusion of the review period, and "shall only apply with respect to a work when an identical copy of that work is not reasonably available in another form."[8] Practical implications of this language include libraries' potential inability either to access the work for review if they have the print equivalent in their stacks or to use screen shots to promote the upcoming new acquisition to users, even after a purchase decision has been made.

Section 404 allows for three copies for archival or replacement purposes, which represents a significant improvement over previous legislation that condoned only a single copy in the latter instance. Archival copies may be produced under the following conditions: the library must own a copy, the text cannot be otherwise available in a digital format, and the digital copies may not be made available to the public outside the library premises. Replacement copies may be digitally produced so long as "the library or archives has, after a reasonable effort, determined that an unused replacement cannot be obtained at a fair price."[9]

The language used in section 404 may run afoul of some existing consortia arrangements, where libraries agree to share responsibility for permanent storage. As libraries have found themselves increasingly short of space, they have devised these sharing agreements to retain permanent, hard copies of materials that are either less frequently used, or more readily available in another format. By agreeing to maintain an assigned subset of the participating collections in the consortia, each library is able to free up much needed space. The DMCA raises several questions in regards to consortia. Do these shared storage agreements translate into shared ownership? If not, then are digital archives of these materials accessible only to the library claiming physical possession of the title? Would this be the case even if the print equivalent could have been legally accessed by any member library? Can a sharing agreement, explicitly stating that the member libraries jointly own the title, overcome this defect? We believe that meticulously drafted sharing agreements can and should contain joint ownership terms, thereby overcoming any ambiguity of the statute itself.

The DMCA in its entirety highlights the revolution caused by technology, which notably, can be and has been abused by both users and copyright holders. Legislation has not been flexible, much less protean enough, to adapt to and address the rapidly changing needs of opposing interests. Each enactment inadvertently has provided a loophole for either users or publishers, and in the current instance, the scales are solidly on the side of the copyright holder. Libraries, unfortunately, have been caught in the crossfire. In this new age, despite their unique purpose in society, libraries tend to be grouped with general "users," who have been designated by publishers as abusers of copyright who should be subject to technological restrictions. The foreseen outcome is that useful databases are more difficult to obtain, and librarians must spend significantly more time negotiating license agreements.

More information on the DMCA, can be found at the following web sites: Association of Research Libraries (ARL), <http://www.arl. org/info/frn/copy/dmca.html>; the ALA, <http://www.ala.org/Content/ NavigationMenu/Our_Association/Offices/ALA_Washington/Issues2/ Copyright1/DMCA__The_Digital_Millenium_Copyright_Act/Default2515. htm>; or the U.S. Copyright Office, <http://www.copyright.gov/reports/ studies/dmca/dmca_study.html>.

Copyright Term Extension Act[10]

One of the most indirectly influential pieces of legislation to libraries is the Sonny Bono Copyright Term Extension Act, hereinafter CTEA, which lengthened copyright protection for 20 years beyond the previously legislated term. While these modifications do not impact libraries' day-to-day operations, they may deter some necessary and logical preservation and space-saving endeavors. Libraries intending to discard or replace deteriorating or infrequently used print materials in the public domain once sent such materials to be microfilmed. This format preserved content, but reduced the physical amount of storage space needed, and in general proved to be a more durable alternative to other media. In the modern age, digitization became an improved, more cost effective way of archiving information. However, under the CTEA, materials that should have been freely available for reprinting or digitization have been made unavailable for such purposes for an additional 20 years.

A hard-fought and narrow exception to this 20-year extension was adopted for libraries as part of the CTEA.[11] In the last 20 years of a copyright term, libraries may digitize the protected materials if a replacement is not available at a reasonable price, the content is not otherwise commercially available, and the copyright holder has not given notice that either of the two previous conditions is true.[12] The exception has both favorable and unfavorable repercussions for libraries. In its most positive incarnation, it permits libraries to digitize materials outside of its existing holdings, thereby facilitating shared and rapid expansion of collections. In a more sober reading, the undefined term "reasonable" is daunting. What may be reasonable for a for-profit institution may not be reasonable for a non-profit academic library; the lack of a clear definition, along with the accompanying threat of litigation, may discourage libraries from projects that they otherwise would have undertaken.

Uniform Computer Information Transactions Act[13]

As of the writing of this article, only two states–Maryland and Virginia–have adopted the Uniform Computer Information Transactions Act, hereinafter UCITA, a uniform commercial law that proposes to regulate the purchase or license of electronic information products.[14] By validating shrink-wrap and click-on licenses, UCITA represents support for one-sided contracts that are traditionally weighted on the publisher's side. Libraries, in general, object to the uniform act not only because it subverts the negotiation process, but also because it authorizes publishers to extend copyright protections beyond the law's original reach. For example, a publisher's shrink-wrap license could require the library to use the purchased software on a single machine or at a designated location. Under these terms, selling or discarding the machine would not permit the user to transfer the software to a replacement machine. In essence, these stipulations would invalidate a common library practice–the circulation of CDs, DVDs, or other digital resources–and potentially increase the costs of maintaining software on library machines.[15]

Fair use is another casualty of UCITA, which permits publishers the freedom to restrict a licensee's access only to viewing the materials; copying, distributing, or sharing the materials with others may be expressly prohibited. Such terms undercut a core mission of libraries, namely, to serve as information-sharing entities. Bottom line, transmitting electronic documents could violate a library's contract with the publisher, even if the print equivalent could be shared through interlibrary loan.

Another potential pernicious use of UCITA occurs when a library and its users are bound by terms that are not fully disclosed at the time of sale of digital or electronic resources. Such click-on licenses are "signed" by the user instead of the library, *after* the purchase has been completed.[16] These licenses proffer a tempting inducement to licensors to sidestep user protections in copyright law; not only are they non-negotiable, but also they deceive the library during the purchasing phase by including hidden restrictions that the library could not have discovered prior to the purchase.

The inability to negotiate licenses at the time of purchase is significant for all involved–publishers, libraries, and users. A resource that would otherwise be acceptable may be rendered useless under the "take it or leave it" click-on terms. With no room to negotiate, the library may choose to sacrifice the purchase; the publisher would lose potential revenue and exposure of the product; and the user would be unable to access the resource. Moreover, because libraries serve a wide variety of clientele, one-size-fits-all click-on licenses cannot adequately meet the specific needs of different libraries. For a university library that serves thousands, channeling all traffic for a resource to a single machine is neither practical nor useful. For example, a database that cannot be used multiple purposes such as interlibrary loan, consortia purposes, or remote access may be less useful than its print equivalent.

Moreover, UCITA provides vendors with a wide berth for dictating license terms that effectively override the doctrine of first sale, which permits a purchaser of a copyrighted work to resell, loan, or "otherwise dispose of possession of that copy."[17] The doctrine of first sale is at the core of library circulation operations, and it countenances the addition of donated materials to library collections. Insofar as digitally created works such as software, CDs, and electronic books are concerned, the materials falling within the umbrella of this doctrine may be of little commercial value as new versions appear on the market, but could be of great value to library users. After all, libraries are training venues for many patrons, and even initial versions of software can serve as tools for introducing products to patrons who might not otherwise have an opportunity to experiment or use them.

It is worth noting that although UCITA's preface clearly excludes an intent to change intellectual property rights,[18] its writers contradict this statement in two ways. First, on exactly the same page as this pronouncement, UCITA states: "[w]hat rights are acquired or withheld depends on what the contract says." When rights are determined solely by the contract, it logically follows that the contract can negate otherwise valid rights, thereby jeopardizing established protections in the copyright laws. Second, although UCITA provides clear choice of law provisions for when it conflicts with Article 9 of the Uniform Commercial Code,[19] unconscionability,[20] public policy,[21] or consumer protection statutes,[22] it fails to mention fair use.

In short, UCITA, although well-intentioned, places few restrictions[23.] on providers, and consequently, the potential for abuse threatens the ability of libraries to provide information and services. Whenever possible in negotiating licenses, libraries should check to see if forum choice dictates a UCITA state. If so, libraries should attempt to change the terms to a more agreeable forum.

More information on UCITA[24] can be found at <http://www.ala.org/washoff/ucita/> or <http://www.arl.org/info/frn/copy/ucitapg.html>.

Current Legislation

At the time of this writing, new legislative proposals serve as evidence that two opposing camps are actively lobbying their causes in the current congress. For example, while the Piracy Deterrence and Education Act of 2003[25] supporters seek greater copyright protection through stiff enforcement, the Public Domain Enhancement Act[26] advocates seek to advance the "public good" cause, facilitating the movement of works into the public domain.

Another bill in the latter camp, the Benefit Authors without Limiting Advancement or Net Consumer Expectations (BALANCE) Act of 2003,[27] attempts to repair flaws found in the DMCA. Specifically, it acknowledges that the DMCA unfairly sanctioned technological restrictions that could be used against both lawful and unlawful access. This bill reiterates the concept of fair use and explicitly states that fair use trumps the DMCA provisions on technology. It contains three sections toward this end: section two, which protects fair use and consumer expectation in the digital world; section four, which addresses digital first sale issues; and section five, which outlines permissible circumvention to enable fair use and consumer expectations.

Summaries of all current copyright legislation as well as past bills (as of the 105th Congress) are available at <http://www.copyright.gov/legislation/>; full text and a detailed history of these bills can be found at <http://thomas.loc.gov>.

CASE LAW

Legislation rarely provides the last word on copyright. Confused and determined parties–both users and copyright holders–have appealed to the courts for clarification and/or affirmation of these intricate laws. A few seminal cases are described below.

Eldred v. Ashcroft, 537 US 186 (2003)

In keeping in line with three retrospective copyright extensions legislated by Congress in 1831, 1909, and 1976, the court in *Eldred* upheld the constitutionality of the Copyright Term Extension Act as it applies to both existing and future copyrights. Although the legislature is constitutionally prohibited from protecting copyright indefinitely, the justices' decision implies that any term short of a perpetual one is permissible. Justice Stevens noted in his dissent that the practical effect of the ruling is an indefinite copyright term; he illustrated this point by noting that only one year's materials have passed into the public domain in the last 80 years.[28]

The majority of the Court discounted the preamble of the copyright clause, which states that copyright should "promote the Progress of Science."[29] Notably, the legislation contradicts that purpose, as protection continues well beyond an author's death. In other words, this increased protection cannot encourage further production by the deceased, nor can it fully exploit the potential creation by allowing others to build on the work.

Eldred is significant to libraries not only for extending copyright for current materials otherwise due to enter the public domain, but also for the principle that Congress may pass additional legislation, at any time, to expand the length of protection for original works. It may do so even if others have relied on previous legislatively determined copyright terms in the creation of a new product or work.[30]

In the first instance, by extending copyright, *Eldred* impacts libraries' acquisitions decisions by "removing" works from the public domain. Since materials without copyright protection can be reprinted, repackaged, or distributed at lower costs, extending copyright terms results in increasing costs to libraries or decreasing accessibility to users. Moreover, decisions to discard or move materials offsite may need to be revisited, as the works slated to be digitized would have produced an alternative for space-hungry libraries.

In the second instance, by validating the repeated extension of copyright, *Eldred* impacts collection development efforts by hampering the ability of libraries to plan for the digital preservation of materials. Libraries typically rely on grants and outside funding in undertaking such projects; the absence of a definitive term as to when materials enter the public domain, or if they will stay in the public domain, renders the acquisition of funding questionable or the efforts to obtain funding useless. Other issues to consider in the aftermath of a copyright extension include addressing the repercussions of digitizing a work that becomes protected by new legislation, developing discard policies that account for the possibility that the materials might later be withdrawn from the public domain, and establishing a clear understanding of the library's distribution rights, if any, under the CTEA.

Several pieces of current legislation, such as the BALANCE Act, were proposed in direct reaction to the *Eldred* decision.

New York Times Co., Inc. v. Tasini, 533 US 483 (2001)

Prior to 1976, freelance authors lost all claims to copyright protection upon transfer of their materials to publishers, including their ability to revise works and submit them to different publishers. To remedy this injustice, the Copyright Act of 1976 divided the rights, endowing publishers with the "privilege of reproducing and distributing the contribution as part of that particular collective work, any revision of that collective work, and any later collective work in the same series."[31] Unless explicitly stated otherwise in the copyright transfer, authors retained their copyright to the individual work. *Tasini* questioned which of these rights was exercised when publishers sold the electronic equivalent of the collective work to database providers. The justices in *Tasini* ruled in favor of the freelance authors, stating that database publication is individual and not collective. Therefore, the database providers and the original publishers had violated copyright.

Tasini presents a striking example of how copyright has failed to evolve with technological developments. In the court's opinion, a database was compared to print and microforms, but databases are functionally as different from print formats as airplanes are from rowboats. The court insisted that the only acceptable form of collective publication was one that mirrored the original print, without making allowances for the functional differences inherent in a database. Even when the electronic data contained was identical to the print, the justices distinguished them from both print and microformats based on the ability to search and retrieve individual articles; they disregarded the fact that users can essentially perform the same act with print or microformat indices. Further, even though the publishers sold the data in whole to the database providers–arguably the same effect as selling the print newspaper–the publisher was still liable for copyright infringement.

The effect of the *Tasini* decision on libraries was immediately evident. It is important to note that although several library associations, including the ALA, the AALL, and the ARL, were cognizant of the impact of the decision on libraries and their historical archiving of information sources, they filed amici briefs in support of the authors. Even in the wake of the decision, libraries hoped that an amicable and equitable agreement would be reached. To shield themselves from future lawsuits, content aggregators such as Lexis and Westlaw,[32] purged freelance articles from their online databases; likewise, Factiva, Dialog, Gale Group, and ProQuest removed content and provided or instituted mechanisms for reporting withdrawn content.[33] In some cases, as with articles appearing on *The New York Times* website, articles were removed, reviewed, and restored after the newspaper ironed out republishing freelance articles online.[34]

As for libraries, the aftermath of *Tasini* resulted in "diminished" holdings induced by sweeping, overnight removal of previously accessible data. *Tasini* highlighted the fragility of not only databases, but also collection development policies that relied heavily on the existence of digital information. Libraries' budgets were also affected; if they wanted to regain access, they would have to determine if the materials were, indeed, available for sale in another format, and then budget-willing, repurchase the materials with the bittersweet knowledge that the missing materials had once been part of an already paid for database. Moreover, since vendors did not remove content in a uniform manner, libraries struggled with the fact that notice to users by database providers varied.[35] In other words, unless users are sufficiently familiar with the *Tasini* ruling and the fallout, they may be unaware that their search results are potentially incomplete. It should be noted, however, that "by the mid- to late 1990s, most publishers had added online-publication rights to their freelance contracts"[36] such that *Tasini*'s reach is retrospective and not prospective.[37]

One of the potentially explosive and unaddressed issues in *Tasini*'s aftermath is whether or not library archiving is at risk. Does the ruling impact the meaning of section 108, title 17 of the *United States Code*? Would electronic preservation violate copyright, if libraries' methods took a collective work and made it searchable? If each article could be individually retrieved, without reference to its companion pages, will libraries have walked into the morass called *Tasini*? The language used by the justices in *Tasini* clearly expresses the thought that such digitization and indexing would indeed violate copyright, as the resulting product—though accessible only to the library's users—would be an impermissible copy of the work.

FUTURE COPYRIGHT CHALLENGES FOR LIBRARIES

Technology presents us with an ever-changing landscape insofar as copyright law is concerned. Where do we go from here? Although it is not possible to predict precisely what the future holds, one thing is certain: libraries must remain actively involved in the copyright debates in order to ensure continuing access to and fair use of information. Aside from planning for the future, libraries can undertake a number of practical measures now, such as inspecting license agreements carefully; making the most of opportunities to negotiate terms with publishers; participating in efforts to educate and lobby Congress on copyright issues as they relate to the information-sharing objective of libraries; reviewing collection development policies to ensure that they not only addresses the possibility of disappearing electronic resources, but also provide an appropriate contingency plan; and whenever feasible and legal, retaining or advocating for an archive of database contents or "perpetual"[38] access.

Furthermore, the library profession needs to understand the impact of legislation not only on libraries, but also on copyright holders. As long as legislation is imbalanced, addressing only one set of wrongs (e.g., infringement on behalf of the copyright holder or content provider), the struggle for equity will continue. Only through discussion and compromise can both users and copyright holders produce meaningful legislation.

REFERENCES

1. Kenneth D. Crews. *Copyright Essentials for Librarians and Educators* (Chicago: American Library Association, 2000): 6.

2. Id., 5.

3. For a detailed examination of the core values of publishers and copyright holders, as well as the resulting conflict, *see* Laura N. Gasaway, "Values Conflict in the Digital Environment: Librarians Versus Copyright Holders" *Columbia-VLA Journal of Law & the Arts* 24, no. 1 (Fall 2000).

4. House Report (Judiciary Committee) No. 94-1476, 94th Cong., 2d sess., September 3, 1976, (to accompany S.22).

5. *Digital Millennium Copyright Act*, *U.S. Statutes at Large* 112 (1998): 2860 codified at *U.S. Code*, Vol. 17, sec. 101 et seq.

6. F. Gregory Lastowka, "Free Access and the Future of Copyright," *Rutgers Computer and Technology Law Journal* 27, no. 2 (2001): 307.

7. *U.S. Code*, Vol. 17, sec. 1201(a). Sec 103.

8. *U.S. Code*, Vol. 17, sec. 1201(d)(2).

9. *U.S. Code*, Vol. 17, sec. 108(c)(1).

10. *U.S. Statutes at Large* 112 (1998): 2827 codified in 17 *U.S. Code*, Vol. 17, sec. 301 et seq. Pub. L. 105-298, 112 Stat. 2827 codified in 17 U.S.C. §301, et seq.

11. *Copyright Term Extension Act*, sec. 104, *U.S. Statutes at Large* 112 (1998): 2827 codified at *U.S. Code*, Vol. 17, sec. 108.

12. *U.S. Code*, Vol. 17, sec. 108.

13. National Conference of Commissioners on Uniform State Laws, Uniform Computer Information Transactions Act (Without Prefatory Notes and Comments), 1999. Online. Internet. Available: <http://www.law.upenn.edu/bll/ulc/ucita/ucita200.pdf> (Reviewed on Aug. 26, 2003).

14. To track the status of UCITA legislation in each state, visit the ALA website at <http://www.ala.org/Content/NavigationMenu/Our_Association/Offices/ALA_ Washington/Issues2/Copyright1/UCITA/UCITA.htm>.

15. Carrie Russell, "Fair Use Under Fire," *Library Journal* 128, no. 13 (August 2003): 32, 33-34. "Recently, Sen. Orrin Hatch (R-UT) made the picture even sound more dire. Hatch suggested that copyright holders who suspected that a citizen is using a copyrighted work in ways not authorized simply be allowed to destroy the user's computer. If that sounds like outrageous talk, it is not. The practice, known as 'self-help,' already exists in some click-on license agreements and has even cropped up in legislation such as UCITA. Thus, if a patron were suspected of illegal activity, the library could very well lose a computer. And even if that patron is ultimately proven innocent, the library may not be able to recover damages under the terms of the license."

16. For a thoughtful explanation and analysis of UCITA, see, Jonathan Franklin, "The Perils of Clicking 'I Agree': UCITA and Intellectual Freedom," *Alki* 19, no. 1 (March 2003): 10-12.

17. *U.S. Code*, Vol. 17, sec. 109(a).

18. National Conference of Commissioners on Uniform State Laws, Uniform Computer Information Transactions Act (With Prefatory Notes and Comments), 2001. Online. Internet. Available: <http://www.law.upenn.edu/bll/ulc/ucita/ucita01.pdf> (Reviewed on Aug. 26, 2003): 2.

19. Uniform Computer Information Transactions Act, sec. 103.

20. Id., sec. 111.

21. Id., sec. 105.

22. Id.

23. There are only two types of restrictions not permitted by UCITA, unconscionable ones and those against public policy. *See* Franklin, 10-11.

24. Id.; James Heller, "UCITA: Still Crazy After All These Years and Still Not Ready for Prime Time," *Richmond Journal of Law & Technology (Online)* 8, no. 1 (Fall 2001). "UCITA not only permits the licensor to change the standards for manifesting assent, but also changes to the contract itself. In fact, an electronic message changing contract terms may be enforceable even if the licensee never receives it."

25. H.R. 2517, 108th Cong., 1st sess. (June 19, 2003).

26. H.R. 2601, 108th Cong., 1st sess. (June 25, 2003).

27. H.R. 1066, 108th Cong., 1st sess. (March 4, 2003).

28. 537 US 186, 123 S. Ct. 769, at 800 (2003).

29. US Const., Art I, sec. 8, cl. 8.

30. "Ex post facto extensions of copyrights result in a gratuitous transfer of wealth from the public to authors, publishers, and their successors in interest." 537 US 186, 123 S. Ct. 769, 793.

31. *U.S. Code*, Vol. 17, sec. 201(c). U.S.C. §201(c).

32. Douglas P. Bickham, "Extra! Can't Read All About It: Articles Disappear After High Court Rules Freelance Writers Taken Out of Context in *New York Times Co. v. Tasini*," *Western State University Law Review* 29, no. 1 (Fall 2001): 100; see also, Scott Carlson, "Once-Trustworthy Newspaper Databases Have Become Unreliable and Frustrating," *Chronicle of Higher Education* 48, no. 20 (January 2002): A30.

"Charles Sims, a lawyer for Lexis-Nexis, says that database has seen similar losses. In many case, he says a citation is left in the article's place, so that people can tell what is missing and be able to look it up on microfilm."

33. Barbara Quint, "*Tasini* Damage-Reporting Decisions," *Information Today* 19, no. 4 (April 2002): 8-12.

34. Carlson, A30. "Toby Usnik, a spokesman for The New York Times, said that since the Supreme Court ruling, in June, the newspaper has pulled 100,000 articles offline; however, 15,000 of those articles have since been restored after the paper struck deals with writers. Mr. Usnick says the paper's management is determined to get all of the articles back online, but he's not certain when that will happen."

35. Carlson. A30.

36. Id., A29.

37. Cristine and Sophia Martins, "Electronic Copyright in a Shrinking World." *Computers in Libraries* 22, no. 5 (May 2002). "From the historical perspective, librarians, archivists, and researchers are justifiably worried that large segments of late 20th century newspaper and magazine articles may become unavailable except through traditional paper-based means. If the digital library is our future- and indeed, our present in many cases-then this could potentially be a very big problem as we cease to have the breadth of access we are used to in online searching."

38. How can a license be perpetual? This descriptive term has been cropping up more frequently in licenses. Generally, these licenses dictate a relatively high upfront cost, coupled with a relatively low maintenance fee for the duration of the database's life. As long as the licensee continues to pay the maintenance fee, its coverage under the license is "perpetual." Bottom line, perpetual licenses are a sticky because most licenses do not initially contain terms detailing maximum increases in license fees. Unless the increases are negotiated in advance, licensors theoretically could raise fees astronomically from one year to the next.

SELECTED RESOURCES

Arlene Bielefield and Lawrence Cheeseman, *Technology and Copyright Law: A Guidebook for the Library, Research, and Teaching Professions* (New York: Neal-Schuman Publishers, Inc., 1997).

Association of Research Libraries, *Copyright, Public Policy, and the Scholarly Community* (Washington, DC: ARL, 1995). This resource references a document, "Fair Use in the Electronic Age: Serving the Public Interest," which is available at <http://arl.cni.org/info/frn/copy/fairuse.html>.

Laura N. Gasaway and Sarah K. Wiant, "Computers, Software, Databases and Copyright," chap. 6 in *Libraries and Copyright: A Guide to Copyright Law in the 1990s* (Washington, DC: Special Libraries Association, 1994): 113-139.

Gretchen McCord Hoffman, *Copyright in Cyberspace: Questions and Answers for Librarians.* (Neal-Schuman Publishers: New York, NY, 2001).

Lawrence Lessig Blog, <http://www.lessig.org/blog/>.

Subscribing to Databases:
How Important Is Depth and Quality
of Indexing?

Linwood DeLong

SUMMARY. This paper compares the subject indexing on articles pertaining to Immanuel Kant, agriculture, and aging that are found simultaneously in Humanities Index, Academic Search Elite (EBSCO) and Periodicals Research II (Micromedia ProQuest), in order to show that there are substantial variations in the depth and quality of indexing in these databases. Libraries that are considering a subscription to a database should pay careful attention to the depth and quality of indexing in making their decisions. *[Article copies available for a fee from The Haworth Document Delivery Service: 1-800-HAWORTH. E-mail address: <docdelivery@haworthpress.com> Website: <http://www.HaworthPress.com> © 2007 by The Haworth Press, Inc. All rights reserved.]*

KEYWORDS. Academic Search Elite, Canada, databases, Humanities Index, Periodicals Research II, subject indexing, University of Winnipeg Library

Linwood DeLong is Reference Coordinator, University of Winnipeg Library, 515 Portage Avenue, Winnipeg, Manitoba, Canada R3B 2E9 (E-mail: l.delong@uwinnipeg.ca).

[Haworth co-indexing entry note]: "Subscribing to Databases: How Important Is Depth and Quality of Indexing?" DeLong, Linwood. Co-published simultaneously in *The Acquisitions Librarian* (The Haworth Information Press, an imprint of The Haworth Press, Inc.) Vol. 19, No. 1/2 (#37/38), 2007, pp. 99-106; and: *Collection Development Issues in the Online Environment* (ed: Di Su) The Haworth Information Press, an imprint of The Haworth Press, Inc., 2007, pp. 99-106. Single or multiple copies of this article are available for a fee from The Haworth Document Delivery Service [1-800-HAWORTH, 9:00 a.m. - 5:00 p.m. (EST). E-mail address: docdelivery@haworthpress.com].

Available online at http://www.haworthpress.com/web/AL
© 2007 by The Haworth Press, Inc. All rights reserved.
doi:10.1300/J101v19n37_08

INTRODUCTION

Libraries that are considering a subscription to an online database often find that there is more than one database that covers a given subject discipline. If two databases cover essentially the same mix of journals, it may be tempting to consider one of them for cancellation. In deciding which databases to select or de-select, one often turns to objective, quantifiable criteria such as the overall number of journals that are indexed, the number of journals in a given discipline or subject area that are covered, the number of years of coverage, the percentage of full text that is available, and whether the full text is in HTML or PDF formats. In their study of full-text databases in relation to print journals, Sprague and Chambers draw attention to factors such as currency, the treatment of figures, tables, formulas and other graphical information, as well as stability of content.[1]

ADDITIONAL CRITERIA

Before making any decisions to cancel or subscribe to a database, one should pay careful attention to an additional set of factors that receive much less attention in database reviews: how thorough is the subject indexing of the journals that are covered by different databases? Are approximately the same number of subject terms applied to an individual article? Is the indexing precise enough to capture the specific topics that are addressed by the article? Is the indexing consistent within the database? Does the database actually index all of the articles that it claims to? In the literature that was reviewed for this study, the importance of indexing is frequently mentioned in passing, but it is not pursued in detail.[2]

METHODOLOGY

To gain some preliminary answers to these questions, approximately eighty articles were selected that are all indexed in the following databases: Humanities Index, Academic Search Elite (EBSCO), and Periodicals Research II (Micromedia ProQuest). The subject terms (including geographic designations and personal names) assigned to each of these articles in each database as well as the brief abstract that is found in individual entries in Academic Search Elite and Periodicals Research II were compared. Although it could be objected that Humanities Index does not contain prose abstracts, this difference enables one to consider how much additional subject access is actually achieved by these added abstracts. Three subject areas were chosen for closer comparison: Immanuel Kant, agriculture, and aging.

THE RESULTS

In the case of the approximately 20 articles pertaining to Kant that were compared, several issues immediately become apparent. In Academic Search Elite, personal names used as subject headings do not include years of birth or death. While this is not a problem for the name Immanuel Kant, it is easy to imagine persons who have the same first name and surname and who might otherwise be confused with each other in a subject search. Humanities Index always includes the birth and death years for Kant and for most of the philosophers who are listed in the subject or descriptor fields, though some person's dates were missing in the entries that were examined (for example the Chinese Marxist philosopher Li Zehou, 1930-). In Periodicals Research II, dates are provided frequently, but inconsistently. More seriously, Kant (or the philosophers he is being discussed with) is often omitted entirely in the subject headings that are provided in both Academic Search Elite and Periodicals Research II. Sometimes his name appears in the abstract, but frequently only in modified forms such as "Kant's," "Kantian" or "neo-Kantian." Furthermore, when the name Kant is applied as a subject heading, there is frequently no indication as to which of his writings is being discussed. In the case of seventeen articles that deal specifically with the *Kritik der Urteilskraft*, only three of the entries in Academic Search Elite and three in Periodicals Research II mention this specific text. While the indexing in Humanities Index was generally better in the articles dealing with Kant, it is noteworthy that in an exchange of articles between Robert Wicks and Paul Guyer in *The Journal of Aesthetics and Art Criticism* concerning Paul Guyer's book *Kant and the Claims of Taste*[3] there is no mention of Guyer as a subject heading in Humanities Index. The subject terms for the same articles in Periodicals Research II contain no mention of Kant; Academic Search Elite is the only database that mentions both Kant and Guyer.

The articles that deal with agriculture illustrate other potential problems in indexing. Many of these articles deal with agriculture during a specific historical period and in a defined location. Thus it is instructive to observe not only how the different databases deal with agricultural terminology but also with these two supplementary issues. The treatment of the article by Martin Bruegel, "Work, gender, and authority on the farm: the Hudson Valley countryside, 1790s-1850s"[4] illustrates these issues. In Humanities Index three subject headings are assigned, "Women-New York State-History," "Agriculture-New York State-History" and " Farm women." The actual location within New York State is missed, as is the time period. In Periodicals Research II the subject headings are more precise regarding the location: "Farming," "Families & family life," "Sex roles," "History" and "Hudson Valley, New York," and the abstract re-states the time period under discussion in the article. The subject headings in Academic Search Elite are far too general: "Sexual division of labor," "Agriculture," "Labor productivity" and "North America," and the abstract neither identifies the place in North America that is being discussed nor the time period: "Focuses on the evolution of sexual division of farm labor in North America. Impact of women exclusion on labor productivity; Influence of culture on defining tasks for women and men; Effect of agricultural development on balance of task." When one observes the indexing of the same article in America: History and Life, a specialized history database produced by the ABC-Clio, one notices not only that the time period and location are clearly stated but also that the abstract provides much more information about the content of the article: the transition from mixed farming to hay and dairy specialization, as well as the impact of commercialization on the roles of women on the farm. The geographic terms used in Academic Search Elite with the articles that deal with agriculture are consistently very broad or in other instances, absent. "United States" is the term used for an article that deals with beans in the northern Eastern Woodlands; articles that deal with cocoa plantations in Sao Tomé and with gardening strategies in North Central New Mexico have no geographic subject term assigned to them.

  Throughout these 30 articles one notices tendencies to rely on abbreviations that many searchers would not use (e.g., "Longview, TX" or "Longview, Tex") or on geographic area designations that are ambiguous. Both Humanities Index and Periodicals Research II use the term "Western states" without further qualification to refer to the western states in the United States (even though Australia also has eastern and western states). Academic Search Elite uses the term "West (U.S.)," followed by "United States." The treatment of agricultural terms is fairly consistent among the three different indexes, although there are occasional surprises. An article with the cryptic title "Mexico's Wonder

Plant,"[5] which is really about the maguey plant, does not receive any explanatory subject heading in Humanities Index. There are only headings dealing with the area where it is grown (Oaxaca) and the people who cultivate it (Zapotec Indians). Both Academic Search Elite and Periodicals Research II identify the "wonder plant." As is to be expected, one finds minor variations in terminology among these databases, such as "cows" and "cattle," "agriculture" and "horticulture," or "land reform" and "agrarian reform." There is no observable consistency in Academic Search Elite, however, between terms that occur in the abstract or article title, and terms that are used as subjects. In an article that deals with climate and diet in the earliest times in the Fremont area near Great Salt Lake,[6] only the subject terms "Agriculture," "Archaeology" and "Corn" are assigned. In many other instances, the subject terms and the words used in the abstract are almost identical.

The 30 articles dealing with aging that were selected reflect subtle differences in approaches to indexing among these three databases. Whereas Humanities Index and Academic Search Elite frequently use terms accompanied by subdivisions, e.g., "Aging–Psychological aspects," "Aging–Social aspects," "Aged–Press coverage," "Aged–Religious life," Periodicals Research II uses terms such as "aging," "aged," or "middle age" without qualifiers, and relies on the use of several different subject headings to convey the equivalent of the subdivision of a topic. The treatment of the article "Death and the Maiden" by Arnold Steinhardt[7] illustrates an interesting problem that database producers face. The title "Death and the Maiden" has been used widely, for motion pictures, plays, books and for a famous string quartet by Franz Schubert. The original name for the string quartet was "Der Tod und das Mädchen." Based on the practice in Humanities Index of quoting the titles of artistic works in their original language, and given the central role of this string quartet in this article, one would expect a subject heading for this string quartet, in German. Since Mr. Steinhardt's article is not only about this quartet but also about a performance of it by the Guarneri Quartet, one would hope to find a subject heading for a musical performance as well as one for a piece of music in the string quartet repertoire. Periodicals Research II does not deal with this issue at all in its subject headings (and in fact does not use "Death and the Maiden" as a subject heading anywhere); Humanities Index uses a more general term for Schubert string quartets ("Schubert, Franz 1797-1828–Work–String quartets"), but does not refer to the title of this specific quartet in English or German. Academic Search Elite uses the term "DEATH & the Maiden (Music release)," and refers to Schubert only in the abstract. It should be possible in these databases to search for discussions of performances or recordings of this work as well as for discussions of it as a piece of music, as subject terms, but none of the three databases allows for all of these possibilities in their subject headings.

Whereas Humanities Index generally refers to works of literature in their original language, Academic Search Elite and Periodicals Research II consistently refer to them in translation. There are arguably advantages and disadvantages to both approaches. If a work of literature does not have an established translated title, the use of the title in the original language will eliminate uncertainty. On the other hand, library users may not be familiar with the title in the original language, and may miss important articles because they search for Kafka's *Trial* rather than *Der Prozess*. Not only should libraries consider the depth and quality of the indexing of articles, they should also consider how much knowledge of foreign languages is assumed within the indexing policies of a database.

GENERAL ISSUES

In addition to peculiarities associated with specific subject areas, there are some general issues that become apparent in a study of this nature. Many articles in Humanities Index are referred to as "review articles," meaning that several texts are discussed. Whereas Academic Search Elite and Periodicals Research II generally provide the author's names and at least part of the titles, the index terms in Humanities Index are deficient. Usually there is no indication which texts are being reviewed; sometimes an author's name is provided. The article entitled "Lewis White Beck on Reasons and Causes,"[8] for example, is actually a discussion of the book *Essays by Lewis White Beck: Five Decades as a Philosopher*, edited by Predag Cicovacki, but the subject heading in Humanities Index is only "Beck, Lewis White, 1913-1997." Many of the articles listed in Periodicals Research II are linked directly to a PDF version of the article, and contain no subject terms or abstract at all. More seriously still, there are numerous instances in which articles, sometimes entire issues of a journal, are omitted in one of the databases, even though it is claimed that the database provides full indexing for a given journal for the year in which the article was published.[9] This is consistent with the research by Sprague and Chambers, who note that there is a significant variation in the availability of major articles among fives databases that they studied, and that online databases generally do not provide cover-to-cover inclusion of the full texts of journals.[10] To this should be added the frequency of mistakes in the spelling of authors' names, making it difficult to conduct reliable searches by author.

CONCLUSION

Clearly there is no such thing as a perfect database. It is hoped that the preceding discussion shows that careful attention should be given to the quality and depth of indexing, when a database is selected and that it is highly desirable to compare the indexing of similar articles among different databases, to determine whether the treatment of personal names, the treatment of non-English titles, the use of geographic designations, and the precision in the application of subject terms is satisfactory for the purpose that the database is to serve. Although it could be argued that the move toward the inclusion of searchable, full texts of articles in databases renders subject searching or controlled vocabulary indexing unnecessary or obsolete, previous research does not support this view. A summary by Jennifer Rowley of the debate concerning controlled vocabulary versus natural language indexing[11] shows that a combination of the two is important to achieve adequate precision and recall, and that reliance on natural language searching of full text databases usually results in low precision or relevance. It should be noted that at least one full-text database, Project Muse, continues to use subject headings to augment the entries for articles because it is essential for reliable and comprehensive user searching, that there be consistent terminology, devoid of inflections or other spelling variations, that is applied consistently, with adequate concern for both broadness and precision, to the articles that are indexed in databases.

REFERENCES

1. Sprague, Nancy and Mary Beth Chambers. "Full-Text Databases and the Journal Cancellation Process: A Case Study." *Serials Review* 26, no. 3 (2000): 19-32.

2. Bates, Marcia. "Indexing and Access for Digital Libraries and the Internet: Human, Database, and Domain Factors." *Journal of the American Society for Information Science* 49 (1998): 1185-1205.

Beaubien, Denise M. "Wilson vs. IAS on Tape: A Comparison." *Database* 15, no. 1 (1992): 52-56.

McDonald, Steve. "Improving Access to the International Coverage of Reports of Controlled Trials in Electronic Databases: A Search of the Australasian Medical Index." *Health Information and Libraries Journal* 19 (2002): 14-20.

Neuzil, Mark. "Gambling with Databases: A Comparison of Electronic Searches and Printed Indices." *Newspaper Research Journal* 15, no. 1 (1994): 44-54.

Nichsolson, Scott. "Indexing and Abstracting on the World Wide Web: An Examination of Six Web Databases." *Information Technology and Libraries* 16, no. 2 (1997): 73-81.

Price, Vince. "Recall, Relevance, and Database Design: The Role of Quality." *Information Today* January, 2003: S4-S5.

Read, Eleanor J. and R. Craig Smith. "Searching for Library and Information Science Literature: A Comparison of Coverage in three Databases." *Library Computing* 19, no. 1-2 (2000): 118-126.

3. Wicks, Robert. "Can Tattooed Faces be Beautiful: Limits on the Restriction of Forms in Dependent Beauty." *Journal of Aesthetics and Art Criticism* 57 (1999): 361-363.

Guyer, Paul. "Dependent Beauty Revisited: A Reply to Wicks." *Journal of Aesthetics and Art Criticism* 57 (1999): 357-361.

4. Bruegel, Martin. "Work, Gender, and Authority on the Farm: The Hudson Valley Countryside, 1790s-1850s." *Agricultural History* 76 (Winter, 2002): 1-27.

5. Feinman, Gary M., Linda M. Nicholas and Helen P. Haines. "Mexico's Wonder Plant." *Archaeology* 55, no. 5 (2002): 32-5.

6. Coltrain, Joan Brenner and Steven W. Leavitt. "Climate and Diet in Fremont Prehistory: Economic Variability and Abandonment of Maize Agriculture in the Great Salt Lake Basin." *American Antiquity* 67 (2002): 453-485.

7. Steinhardt, Arnold. "Death and the Maiden." *Yale Review* 86, no. 4 (1998): 64-78.

8. Guyer, Paul. "Lewis White Beck on Reasons and Causes" *Journal of the History of Ideas* 63 (2002): 539-545.

9. Hughes, Benije. "Apples to Oranges: The Semanticist in Scientific Clothing." *Etc.* 58, no. 4 (Winter, 2001/2002): 396-399 is not indexed in Academic Search Elite, even though the article is present in PDF format. Both Humanities Index and Periodicals Research II list this article. Issue 290 of the journal *Antiquity* (2001) is completely missed in Academic Search Elite.

10. Sprague and Chambers, "Full-Text Databases and the Journal Cancellation Process" *Serials Review* 26, no. 3 (2000): 20, 26-27.

11. Rowley, Jennifer. "The Controlled versus Natural Indexing Languages Debate Revisited: A Perspective on Information Retrieval Practice and Research." *Journal of Information Science* 20 (1994): 108-119.

Annual Reports:
Preserving and Disseminating
a Source for Business History

Cynthia L. Cronin-Kardon
Michael Halperin

SUMMARY. Lippincott Library's Historical Corporate Annual Reports Collection contains useful primary sources of information for several disciplines, including applied accounting and business history. They also are reflections of the societal and cultural mores of the times. Unfortunately, these reports are fragile, difficult to locate, and hard to access. The creation of a digital collection preserves images of the reports and makes them easily accessible for anyone with access to the Internet. This paper details the efforts of Lippincott Library at the University of Pennsylvania to create an electronic collection of historical annual reports based on a large print collection owned by the library. The challenges of electronic "preservation" are discussed, as well as possible solutions. *[Article copies available for a fee from The Haworth Document Delivery Service: 1-800-HAWORTH. E-mail address: <docdelivery@haworthpress.com> Website: <http://www.HaworthPress.com> © 2007 by The Haworth Press, Inc. All rights reserved.]*

Cynthia L. Cronin-Kardon is Document Delivery Librarian (E-mail: croninkc@wharton.upenn.edu); and Michael Halperin is Director (E-mail: halperin@wharton.upenn.edu), both at the Lippincott Library, University of Pennsylvania, Philadelphia, PA 19104.

[Haworth co-indexing entry note]: "Annual Reports: Preserving and Disseminating a Source for Business History." Cronin-Kardon, Cynthia L., and Michael Halperin. Co-published simultaneously in *The Acquisitions Librarian* (The Haworth Information Press, an imprint of The Haworth Press, Inc.) Vol. 19, No. 1/2 (#37/38), 2007, pp. 107-118; and: *Collection Development Issues in the Online Environment* (ed: Di Su) The Haworth Information Press, an imprint of The Haworth Press, Inc., 2007, pp. 107-118. Single or multiple copies of this article are available for a fee from The Haworth Document Delivery Service [1-800-HAWORTH, 9:00 a.m. - 5:00 p.m. (EST). E-mail address: docdelivery@haworthpress.com].

Available online at http://www.haworthpress.com/web/AL
doi:10.1300/J101v19n37_09

KEYWORDS. Business history, corporate histories, digitizing, Internet, preservation, Lippincott Library, University of Pennsylvania, Wharton School, World Wide Web

INTRODUCTION

Academic business libraries often house large collections of historical annual reports on paper. The Wharton School's Lippincott Library at the University of Pennsylvania, for example, has an annual report collection containing some 45,000 annual reports with more than 3 million pages. These collections, with reports dating back to the early nineteenth century, have the potential for allowing business historians to research the development and growth of business and industries. The reports are useful to scholars in several historical sub-disciplines.

Some examples:

History of Accounting and Finance

Accounts form the centerpiece of corporate annual reports. As a consequence, they are primary documents in the history of applied accounting. At the Wharton School, annual reports from the 1940s were used by researchers to describe the early use of stock options. In addition, using a collection housed at the Bruno Business Library at the University of Alabama, William D. Samson and Gary John Previts used historical reports for the B&O Rail Road to research the company's elevation of accounting as an effective tool in decision making. More recently they, as well as Dale L. Flesher, used these reports and other sources to examine the use of auditing well before the existence of any regulatory requirements.

History of Graphic Design and Advertising

Annual reports often use innovative graphic designs. The 1963 Eastman-Kodak report featuring a 3-D cover is a classic example. The photographic inserts used by the Container Corporation's annual reports from 1936-1949 were obtained from the Lippincott collection and were featured in an exhibition by the Cooper-Hewitt Museum (the Smithsonian Institution's National Museum of Design). In 1994, an article appeared in *Across the Board* that examined the changing role of annual reports, from mere financial statements to marketing tools and advertising vehicles. In the 1950s, IBM hired a graphic designer; the look of annual reports has never been the same. In fact, there are now newsletters and awards devoted to design excellence in annual reports.

The cover page of the 1950 Hudson Motor Car Company's report visually demonstrates to the public the modern look and universal appeal of the company's product. In the color illustration, the sky is blue, the colors are fresh, and the image gives the impression that one could go anywhere in a Hudson car (Figure 1).

History of Technology

Early annual reports (before 1850) sometimes include descriptions and schematic drawings of machines. This material can be a valuable complement to the more formal descriptions in patent literature. The rail diagram in Figure 2 is an example.

Social, Political, and Economic History

Annual reports are a largely untapped source for social, political, and economic history. Reporting on the key issues of the day, they are an archive of the American industrial experience. More than a window on the development of corporate America, the reports give us insights on the cultural, historical, and societal mores of the country. Reports from war years (the Civil War, and the First and Second World Wars) describe the impact of war on companies and on the economy: the changed workforce, the allocation of materials for war-related products, and the resulting discontinuance of other products (like nylon stockings). They can also impart a sense of the emotional toll, sacrifice, and patriotism of the country. A president's letter to stockholders is filled with support for "the boys over there" in rhetoric and in descriptions of a company's contributions to the war effort. The annual report of the Baltimore & Ohio Rail Road Company for 1863 includes detailed descriptions of the company's bridges, trestles, track, and engines which were destroyed by the Confederate Army. The 1831 report includes firsthand accounts of a strike by laborers over non-payment of wages (Figure 3).

Railroad company annual reports not only detail the development of the transportation industry, but they also provide a picture of the growth of the nation and its movement westward. This is documented by the descriptions of the numbers and locations of track laid. It is further supported through examination of the inventories of products transported

FIGURE 1. Hudson Motor Car Company Annual Report 1950

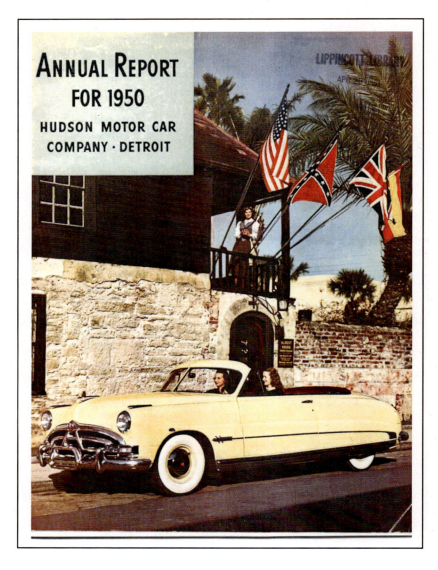

FIGURE 2. Rail Diagram: Baltimore and Ohio Rail Road 1834

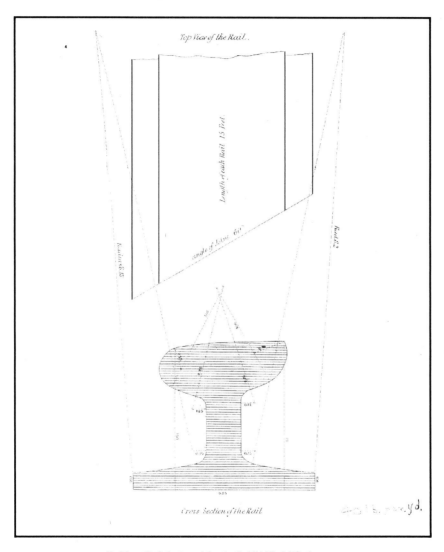

Rolled Iron Rail designed for the Balt? & Wash? Railway .

FIGURE 3. Excerpt from Baltimore & Ohio Rail Road 1831 Annual Report, Describing a Riot by Striking Workmen Over Lack of Payment

45

they refused to accept any thing less than the whole amount due to them from Lyon.

To their demand of full payment Mr. Stabler could only answer that he came there for a specific purpose, to distribute a certain sum, and if they declined taking it, he must return to Baltimore for further orders. Seeing that nothing could be obtained from Mr. Stabler the workmen marched directly to the road, armed with their usual tools, and commenced destroying the sills, and tearing up the culverts in the neighbourhood of Sykes'. After a short time however, they were induced to cease, and agreed to wait until ten o'clock the next day,—in the hope that what they had already done, would bring the board to terms with them ; determining if it failed, to continue to commit acts of violence until they succeeded in obtaining full payment. Mr. Stabler came express to Baltimore where he arrived at 2 o'clock on the 29th and calling at once upon the counsel of the company, a warrant was obtained from Judge Hanson, requiring the Sheriff to arrest the persons named in it, and all others whom he might find engaged in the riot. This was put in the Sheriff's hands at three o'clock, with directions that he should at once proceed to the spot, summoning as he went the *"Posse comitatus"* and endeavour to keep the peace and support the laws. The Sheriff reached the 3d Division on the next morning, Thursday, in company with Mr. Patterson the only person of the *Posse* who attended to his summons at that time. They had not proceeded far down the road when they were met by the workmen to the number of 135 marching with their stone hammers, and other tools, with a handkerchief on a pole for a flag, under the command of one of their number, named Hugh Reily, to whom they appeared to pay implicit obedience. One of them seized the reins of the Sheriff's horse and refused to let him proceed, and *all* were totally regardless of his authority, and injunctions. Finding that he was powerless to protect the laws, he returned to Sykes' and dispatched an express to Baltimore, stating the inefficiency of the civil authority without the assistance of a strong armed force.

The conjuncture had now arrived, when for the first time it became legal to call for military aid, and within an hour after the express reached town, Judge Brice had granted the necessary warrant to Brigadier General Steuart, and by ten o'clock on Thursday night, upwards of 100 of the volunteer troops of this city, fully equipped and officered were despatched in cars to the aid of the Sheriff. They reached the 3d Division, soon after from one area to another. These inventories also highlight the preferences and needs of the consumer at different times in history.

UNREALIZED RESEARCH POTENTIAL

The research potential of historical annual reports is largely unrealized, because the reports as paper documents have several limitations:

Local Availability

Lippincott Library, as is the case among its peer business school libraries, is the sole repository of historical annual report materials for a large geographic region. Rare or unique reports are rarely loaned by institutions. The fact that researchers have to "go to the documents" severely limits their use as primary sources for scholars.

Lack of Search Aids

Historical annual report collections often are not indexed. Even using the best-indexed annual report collection, the researcher can usually find little more than the company name and the year in which the report was published.

Deteriorating Condition

Annual report collections often contain rare or unique reports. Unfortunately, this material will be lost without some preservation program. Within Lippincott's collection, many reports, even those from the 1940s and 1950s, are already at risk of total deterioration. Pages can hardly be touched or turned without tearing or crumbling. As with their contemporary publications, many annual reports were printed on highly acidic paper which will eventually self-destruct.

PUTTING THE REPORTS ON THE WEB

To address these problems, we decided in 1997 to scan a selection of annual reports and make them available on the Web (http://scripts.library. upenn.edu/cgi-bin/corprep/recordList). The Library received a grant from the Price Waterhouse Company, which allowed the project to begin. Generous support from Joseph Lippincott III has insured that the program will continue. Three divisions of the Penn Library System were involved in the project: the Lippincott Library; the Schoenberg Center for Electronic Text & Image, or SCETI (http://dewey.library. upenn.edu/sceti/); and the Penn Library Systems Department.

SCETI handled the actual scanning of the documents, and also the optical character recognition (OCR) processing using Adobe Acrobat. A database was created using Verity software to make the collection Web searchable. Lippincott was involved in providing the materials, and with inputting appropriate tags and identifiers to help with keyword searching and consistency in the records. The Penn Library Systems Office provided technical backup.

Initially, we chose company reports from a variety of industries. We focused initially on two periods in American history: World War II and the Depression. Finally, we decided not to use colored images in order to limit fill size and insure faster loading.

As SCETI became more involved in other projects, Lippincott has taken on more of this project. All of the processing of the reports is now done by the Lippincott Electronic Delivery Service, the primary function of which is to provide Wharton faculty with digitized documents. The Penn Library Systems Department has also taken on a larger role. While Acrobat Capture 3.0 is still the software behind the digitizing and OCR processing, Systems staff have created an Oracle database to index and search the documents as a collection. The collection now has its own server space dedicated to the project. New technologies have allowed us to create better images; some reports now have color images.

PROCESSING THE REPORT

There are two processes required to make a searchable report image. The first process changes a picture of a page into a PDF file, and the second creates an underlying text file that can be searched. The combined operation is time consuming. It takes an average of 5 hours to complete a report. If there are a large number of graphics or more than 30 pages, a report can take days to complete. In addition, any report graphics may need additional processing.

Images are first scanned and edited for imperfections, such as stray marks, using either Paint Shop Pro or Photoshop, two programs with somewhat different features. Graphics may be removed, to be re-inserted into the page at a later time. Adobe Capture 3.0 is then used to process the scanned images into PDF files with searchable text. Adobe Capture allows us to create an automated progression of required steps (a "workflow") so that image files, mostly TIFs, can be submitted and automatically go through the steps required to produce a searchable PDF. Any number of pages can be processed at the same time. The images are broken into separate parts and are run through an OCR process that tries to recognize letters and words. Before the images are finally turned into PDFs, the OCR function includes two steps: "Quick Fix" and "Review Document." They allow for the correction of any "suspect" or unidentified words or characters on the image. Finally, the documents are stored in a folder as PDF files. Any graphics that may have been removed are re-inserted into the PDF file. The result is a fully searchable electronic duplicate of the original paper document. We have outlined the process in Figure 4.

ISSUES INVOLVED WITH DIGITIZING

While the mechanics of scanning pages, processing images, and mounting files may seem straightforward, there were several issues that needed to be addressed. These ranged from logistics (e.g., how to transport printed reports from a remote storage site to the library and back again) to such editorial decisions as the levels of acceptable OCR, the

FIGURE 4. Work Flow Chart

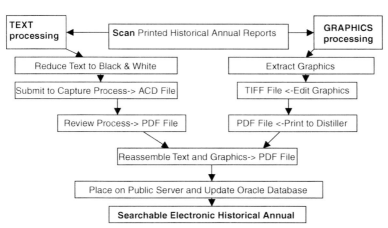

use of color versus black and white, the use of image versus text, and the degree of clarity required.

Scanning

The scanning process was the first problem. It is possible to initiate scanning through Adobe Capture so that this step is part of the auto-mated workflow. However, we quickly discovered that this limited our ability to set scanning options, and produced pages requiring a substantial amount of correction after the OCR process. There might be over 300 suspect words per page in a 24-page report.

While adding a separate stage to the process, it was apparent that it was much more efficient to scan documents into Paint Shop Pro or Photo Shop. Color tones, any skewing of the image, and random marks on the image (from water marks or paper folds on the original document) could be quickly and easily fixed. This helped to significantly reduce the amount of incorrect text later on. The original condition and format of the report dictates how quickly and easily adjustments can be made. For instance, oversize maps or pages need to be either reduced in order to fit on the scanner, or scanned in portions and then put together. Torn pages and fading print also complicated matters, as do pages which combine black-and-white text and colored images.

Color versus Black and White

The decision to use color or black and white is directly related to the condition of the original document. Color can create a truer image of the reports, and provide additional information relating to taste and techno-logical developments in publishing. However, color images also show every water drop, wrinkle or other sign of age; and often obscure the text as well. Color image files are also much larger (39 kilobytes for an average black-and-white page versus 1 megabyte or more for color). Color files may require a higher dpi (dots per inch), and the color palette needed is larger. Color scanning also requires much more preparation time per document as each image might need to have settings individually adjusted. On the other hand, gray-scale and black-and-white scanning often obscures important details on a page, especially if the original is in color.

To save time on later color adjustments and to control file size, as well as to create cleaner images, we often initially scan in color and extract any graphics. Then the text-image is reduced to black and white for

OCR. Finally, any color graphics are re-inserted. This has enabled us to create a document that is small enough to load fairly quickly across the Web, while retaining many of the characteristics of the original print document. The file size of a report can be reduced from 10 megabytes for a full-color report to 3 megabytes.

Image Resolution

A related issue is image resolution. The higher the resolution, the longer the scanning time required and the bigger the file. On the other hand, the higher the resolution, the less time required for cleaning up the text in the OCR process. For instance, a document at lower resolution may have 150 "suspect words," such as "lcconnotwe" for locomotive" or "aml" for "and," versus 30 at a higher resolution. Because of this a mid-range dpi (400) was chosen for most reports, but those in a more deteriorated condition are generally scanned at 600 dpi.

OCR Process

The OCR process creates other challenges. The time needed to correct suspect words and fonts increases with the age of the document. Unlike today's annual reports, which have common fonts, older reports may include type sets that are no longer in use, making character recognition very difficult. This results in many processed pages with misspelled words and a mixture of inconsistent fonts. To reduce the amount of correction required, we limit the number of fonts that the program uses to two: Times New Roman and Arial. While these may not have been the actual fonts of the original report (fonts which we are unlikely to have anyway), they create a clean and consistent image with few errors.

Financial statements are particularly difficult for the OCR program. The numbers are hard to resolve and the fonts often change from line to line. We decided to save financial statement pages as graphics because it would be unlikely for someone to search them for a particular dollar amount. The text headings are still searchable, so it is easy to locate specific statements.

File Size

We have optimized the PDF files for Web browsing so that a report can load and be readable at the same time. Larger reports may be broken into sections to minimize loading time. Reducing individual file size also conserves server space. However, a file can only be reduced so much before it loses searchability or readability. The online collection, when completed, will be about 150 gigabytes. At present, files range from 2 megabytes to 14 megabytes. Additional space is needed for backup files.

Accessibility

Finally, how do we incorporate such a collection into the library holdings? At this time, the collection is not cataloged, but links are available from the Lippincott Library Website. We hope to catalog the collection as a whole and link it to the OPAC.

CONCLUSION

Lippincott Library's Historical Corporate Annual Reports Collection provides a unique perspective on the history, sociology, and economic development of the United States. Fragile documents are being made accessible to anyone with access to the Internet. The library is protecting, preserving, and displaying a large set of documents in an expandable virtual space. As technology advances and we become more proficient with the tools at our disposal, it should be easier and faster to reach our goal.

We wish to thank Delphine Khanna (Digital Project Librarian), Greg Bear (Information Systems Designer, Rare Books and Manuscripts Library), and Richard King (Systems Technician, Lippincott Library) for their invaluable help in creating and operating the Historical Corporate Annual Reports site. We would also like to thank Ellen Slack for her help in editing and reviewing this manuscript.

REFERENCES

Flesher, Dale L., William D. Samson, and Gary John Previts. 2003. The origins of value-for-money auditing: The Baltimore and Ohio railroad: 1827-1830. *Managerial Auditing Journal* 18: 374-386.

R. P. 1994. A history of 'Malicious Obedience.' *Across the Board* 31: 22.

Samson, William D. and Gary John Previts. 1999. Reporting for Success: The Baltimore and Ohio railroad and management information, 1827-1856. *Business and Economic History* 28: 235-248.

FUTURE ISSUES

Enhanced Online Access Requires Redesigned Delivery Options and Cost Models

David Stern

SUMMARY. Rapidly developing online information technologies provide dramatically new capabilities and opportunities, and place new responsibilities on all involved to recreate networks for scholarly communication. Collaborations between all segments of the information network are made possible and necessary as we attempt to find a balanced and mutually beneficial way to maximize these new technologies. This is a time of paradigm change in information delivery that calls for new approaches and considerations. Some of the important new options that require consideration are: the delivery of unbundled and integrated media materials; the recognition and appropriate separation of the costs for

David Stern is Director of Science Libraries and Information Services, Kline Science Library, 219 Prospect Street, PO Box 208111, New Haven, CT 06520-8111 (E-mail: david.e.stern@yale.edu).

[Haworth co-indexing entry note]: "Enhanced Online Access Requires Redesigned Delivery Options and Cost Models." Stern, David. Co-published simultaneously in *The Acquisitions Librarian* (The Haworth Information Press, an imprint of The Haworth Press, Inc.) Vol. 19, No. 1/2 (#37/38), 2007, pp. 119-134; and: *Collection Development Issues in the Online Environment* (ed: Di Su) The Haworth Information Press, an imprint of The Haworth Press, Inc., 2007, pp. 119-134. Single or multiple copies of this article are available for a fee from The Haworth Document Delivery Service [1-800-HAWORTH, 9:00 a.m. - 5:00 p.m. (EST). E-mail address: docdelivery@haworthpress.com].

delivery which are distinct from those of peer review and format-ting/branding; the rationale and means of presenting additional flexible and customizable cost models based upon a variety of factors; and the possible role for agents in developing standardized product packages. This article attempts to highlight some important areas for focused attention, and discusses the responsibilities for proactive input by librarians in these early design considerations. *[Article copies available for a fee from The Haworth Document Delivery Service: 1-800-HAWORTH. E-mail address: <docdelivery@haworthpress.com> Website: <http://www.HaworthPress.com> © 2007 by The Haworth Press, Inc. All rights reserved.]*

KEYWORDS. Cost models, differential pricing, integrated media, on-line information capabilities, peer review, publisher packages, purchasing agents, scholarly communication, unbundled materials

ALTERNATIVE ACCESS METHODS

The rapidly evolving interfaces and overlays (i.e., MetaLib, EnCompass, WebFeat, etc.) and linking technologies (OpenURL applications such as SFX) create new possibilities that demand new access mechanisms and policies. New infrastructures will need to address the underlying complexities of accessing newly "unbundled" materials. These new systems must support entirely new technical and cost model concerns. The newly designed services should both enhance the current delivery options and satisfy the changing demands for a radically new scholarly communications network. This revised set of options should accommodate new unbundled options such as simultaneous access to a wide variety of materials (i.e., journals, continuations, books, reference data), the integration of multi-media materials, and seamless cross-publisher access. Cross-publisher access could be offered through agent profiles, based upon increasing levels of research depth across predefined subject aggregations and interdisciplinary coverage plans. There should be a move away from the standard Big Deal toward the development of Flexible Deals.

The new technical capabilities of unbundled services require a serious redesign of existing information products and the development of entirely new services. The early design of these new models should consider the long-term economic viability of the industry, and should be based upon reasonable, customized, and dynamic user expectations.

Collaboration between information producers, providers, intermediaries, and users will be necessary in order to build practical and well-designed systems that will allow for seamless integration and the assimilation of future enhancements. New value propositions need to be defined and developed into redesigned services and cost models.

WHY CHANGE THE INFRASTRUCTURE?

In addition to the current economic scenario which is creating a need for revised options, new technological enhancements provide significant service modifications including the online delivery of unbundled materials in a much less expensive and more customized manner. These new options must be incorporated into the present models. Of course there are associated costs and concerns that must also be addressed in this new environment such as facilitating the implementation and continuing development of these complex tools and finding adequate archiving solutions.

Important areas for reconsideration due to this new technology include: the separation of peer review from distribution, the redesign of deliverable products after reviewing the value provided for dollars spent, the implementation of evidence-based cost models, and the development of customized profile plans as opposed to the generic Big Deal discount plans. The new unbundled possibilities allow us to reconsider the present service and cost models, and to develop more accountable and reasonable systems that allow for and encourage analysis, flexibility, and customization. Through analysis we will remove the automatic acceptance of existing models and costs, and provide incentives for developing new models.

HOW TO MAKE THESE NEW SYSTEMS INTEGRATE

Integration has been accomplished through a combination of federated and broadcast search technologies and linking techniques. Searching has either been performed on pre-created and centralized indexes or through simultaneous searching of multiple search engines. The greatest challenge has been in developing interoperability through sophisticated search syntax normalization (i.e., MetaLib, EnCompass, WebFeat, etc.). Linking between systems is accomplished through pointing to identified objects or search engines. Appropriate copy concerns have been the largest challenge when dealing with multiple manifestations and versions of targets (i.e., Ovid or PubMed host platforms, html or pdf documents).

New database frameworks will soon make it possible to develop significantly more powerful integration options. These new systems (i.e., FEDORA and OpenURL 2.0) allow researchers to explore deep relationships recorded in very sophisticated object databases. The new infrastructures both describe items and identify their associated actions. This means objects can now be analyzed and manipulated in entirely new ways based upon characteristics of their properties and relationships to other information within their defined communities.

Imagine a search system in which an item (automobile muffler) can be compared to similar task-specific tools within an industry (motorcycle noise abatement pipes) and also to related objects in other fields (a water buffer in a home heating unit). Also imagine that these objects can be compared in terms of price, supplier, delivery time, and many other characteristics. These multi-directional and action-oriented connections can provide new layers of integration through uncovering and displaying relationships between initially isolated items.

For more information on these two link-enabling tools see:

- FEDORA–Open-Source Digital Repository Management System
  <http://www.fedora.info/>
- The OpenURL Framework: origins, evolution, concepts
  <http://wotan.liu.edu/~cescco/OpenURL_day_2003/OpenURL_day_2003.html>

In terms of new uses in the information industry, imagine this enhanced database framework describing traditional published materials at deeper levels such as: added-value captions for images and charts, identifying techniques used in analyses, and multiple resolutions of images for quality considerations. Now also imagine this system incorporating this deeper type of data from materials not previously indexed-such as chapters in books or book series, or even images in books. Links could be made across these materials based upon related concepts, among related images, and even including multi-media (e.g., sound bytes). This deeper integration could result in unified search results appearing from materials originally found in journals, books, encyclopedias, raw data sets, and image files. This "unbundled" material must be packaged in terms of access options and payment schemes.

This expanded access could even cross the gap between published and free material (e.g., web items). In addition to developing intuitive search and display tools, another major challenge to any broad-based integration tool will be developing a way to normalize subject headings and keywords across communities with different vocabularies.

LIBRARIANS SHOULD BE ACCOUNTABLE, RESPONSIBLE, AND INVOLVED

How involved should librarians, authors, readers, and administrators be in determining the design of the new information networks? It is part of our professional responsibility to act as both stewards of intellectual content and as collaborators on future information networks in order to address these new possibilities in more creative and proactive ways. There are serious problems with the current system which these new technologies might address. We should begin by exploring and modifying the underlying causes rather than merely treating the obvious but superficial symptoms with short term fixes. It is time we state for the record where long-term solutions conflict with current activities and special interest concerns. Let us explore some of the major areas demanding librarian input and collaboration.

It is time that librarians join the rest of the professions and support their [purchasing] decisions for both serials and monographs using evidence-based factors. Selectors must be accountable for their short-term actions and the long-term implications of these decisions. The advent of online options creates new possibilities and requires new approaches to creating, distributing, archiving, and manipulating digital materials. New infrastructures, cost models, and purchasing plans must be developed to allow for maximum flexibility based upon local needs. Librarians, along with service vendors and users, should be involved in the early design stages of the new plans rather than serve as sounding boards for previously created plans that primarily address economically advantageous models for publishers.

At what level should journals continue to provide substantial profits to commercial publishers . . . especially considering that continuing this commercial profit skimming at current levels certainly endangers the long-term viability of the entire peer review information distribution mechanism? Should not-for-profit publishers be treated differently than for-profit publishers–and what are the long-term implications of these types of decisions? Should not-for-profit users be charged the same amount as commercial users, or should there be some type of differential pricing? The new differential pricing models need to be re-examined from both the profit side as well as from the user perspective. What factors contribute to the realistic scale of problems, and should short-term and long-term solutions be focused on addressing aspects of commercial and society publishing equally?

Librarians must seriously question the traditional distribution models and their underlying requirements and demands. In these desperate fiscal times for libraries, is it reasonable for organizations to continue treating "freely" provided academically created information as a commodity? Should we simply accept the newly provided ebook and electronic reference cost models as valid without reviewing the underlying basis for these approaches? Are there new ways to provide peer review, editing, distribution, and archiving of academic materials in a more efficient way using new online technologies? Should we continue to simply use traditional journal subscriptions to "subsidize" the academic promotion and tenure process, or are there alternative cost models and infrastructures that are worth exploring?

Promotion and Tenure

A major issue we must address is the pressure for publication within the academic promotion and tenure (P&T) process, and the strain this places on the existing journal distribution model. A similar but less economically difficult strain exists within the book publishing domain. As a result of the "professionalization" of academia, over time the journal distribution mechanism has become the primary way to demonstrate expertise in a field, through either publishing articles or serving on editorial boards. As the number of academic institutions and researchers grow over time there is an ever-increasing need for new outlets for publication and editorial review process activities. In addition, the adoption of automation means that academic research produces an exponential growth in the amount of data that is produced and needs to be published. Due to these factors the expansion of current journals and the proliferation of niche journals have been adding to the size (and therefore the cost) of journals for years.

The indisputable fact is that an important measure of P&T success is based upon this ability to prove "value" through the current publication process. This has created a situation in which the packaging and delivery of the free academic material (and not the material itself) is now treated as the commodity. The organizations that pay for this distribution network have allowed the distributors to set market costs without demanding these costs be related to either actual distribution costs or demonstrable P&T market pressure "values." It seems that over time the distributors have continually emphasized and charged a great deal more for the "P&T value" than for distribution costs. This explains the escalating costs which have little causal relationship to the actual distribution costs.

As long as there was no other way to reasonably distribute these freely provided materials while at the same time documenting professional value (through an acceptable peer-review system) it was difficult to imagine an alternative scholarly communication and recognition system. Certainly the distribution needs had become far too complex and expensive to function as it did in the beginning, as an altruistic network of scholars working for better distribution rather than commercial profit. It was only logical that some form of cost-recovery and/or profit generating system be developed to maintain this paper distribution network. However, new Internet-based distribution mechanisms allow for less expensive and more rapid delivery. Peer review can now be accomplished with less cost, lag time, and infrastructure support than ever before. Perhaps it is now possible to remove (or at least reduce) the impact of commercial packaging and delivery from the system.

Even society and not-for-profit publishers divert a portion of their revenue to fund non-publication interests. Often publicity, educational programming, and other projects are subsidized by publication revenues. This amounts to indirect (and hidden) funding from the taxpayer base, and perhaps this historical funding stream needs to be re-evaluated as we develop new long-term funding priorities and alternative revenue bases.

Alternative Distribution and Peer Review Options

An important first step in analyzing alternatives is to determine if there are any other distribution models that might serve as well and be less expensive to maintain. Eprint servers using OAI protocols are now distributing thousands of manuscripts a day all over the world at a fraction of the cost of paper distribution. Most of these systems do not include a peer review overlay, but it is possible to integrate the current paper peer review process and at the same time adopt online enhancements such as imbedded editorial commentaries, metadata links, and automatic citation awareness services. There are already society-based publications that produce their journal "copy of record" as online journals using these new and improved peer review tools (i.e., Physical Review-STAB and Optics Express). While there is a learning curve for authors and editors, the advantages include much better turnaround time and interactive reviewing. An example of a new manuscript submission and review process tool is the American Chemical Society's Paragon peer review software <https://paragon.acs.org/paragon/index.jsp>.

One could also imagine using these OAI systems to create online clearinghouses of best practices and supporting materials in both peer review and non-reviewed categories. Image an expanded online version of the ERIC Clearinghouse for educational materials. Online distribution of documents on demand would replace the automatic and costly distribution of all accepted materials whether or not they were ever to be used. The idea of moving from just-in-case to on-demand distribution would mean an incredible savings in delivery, local inventory, and storage costs. The archival aspects would be handled far more efficiently using a few clearinghouses which would serve as mirror sites for protection and network efficiency.

Value for Dollars?

Other important questions within a significant review of the entire process are: How do we identify and best support only the truly required tasks within the scholarly communication and peer review process? Are there paper-based tasks that are no longer necessary or worthy of support in these tight fiscal times? Have we adequately forced the investigation of less expensive ways to accomplish some tasks in an online environment? Are there new tasks that require additional funding? Tough questions must be asked; it is no longer possible to accept these escalating costs without demanding and participating in a review and revision of the entire process. For example, are glossy and branded publisher fonts and layouts worth the high cost of commercial distribution? It is time for the purposeful abandonment of certain traditional services and values . . . and for the reallocation of revenue in new ways for less expensive and alternative services. These infrastructure decisions should be based upon the long-term requirements for scalable and extensible scholarly distribution networks.

Now that we have the ability to monitor actual use by organizations, basic service costs should be determined by charging a differential "base fee" to all users to subsidize basic services, plus supplemental charges for any enhanced services based upon local use and other priorities. For many tools, differential pricing based upon vested interest and use seems to be a way of creating fair and reviewable cost models. Obviously, some types of general use tools will not require such complex costing and tracking mechanisms.

Tools for Accountability

If we are to be responsible for providing the best material at the most reasonable cost, we will need evidence-based criteria on which to base these decisions. Librarians have been analyzing use data for years in order to monitor paper materials, but the analysis of online tools has been difficult due to less than desirable statistics across the industry. This was expected in the early stages of the online era, but we are now moving into a more stable phase in which analysis standards need to be developed.

One significant effort to provide standardized online use data is found at the Counting Online Usage of Networked Electronic Resources (COUNTER) initiative. The stated intention is to serve librarians, publishers, and intermediaries by facilitating the recording and exchange of online usage statistics. COUNTER is initially focusing on a core of well-accepted definitions and content structures for journals and databases. "To comply with Release 1 of the COUNTER Code of Practice, vendors will have to provide to customers the set of basic usage reports identified in the Code of Practice as 'Level 1.' In addition to the Level 1 reports, those vendors who can provide the more detailed Level 2 reports will be encouraged to do so, and to make every effort to use the COUNTER definitions in any other usage statistics they may provide to particular customers" <http://www.projectcounter.org/>.

Additional types of use data will need to be developed and analyzed if we are to consider use-based customized and differential pricing. A number of other initiatives are pointed to from the bottom of the COUNTER page.

Other customized and differential pricing models have been developed without use-based criteria. Many of these approaches are based upon supposed correlations between organizational characteristics and projected use. These variables include the research levels of the organization (American Physical Society journals pricing), the productivity of the users (American Mathematical Society database pricing), and the FTE of the organization (many database tools). These types of models need to be explored and further implemented, for while they do create additional complications for vendors and libraries, they do provide a

reasonable and fair price based upon easily identified local considerations.

Another option to be considered in dire circumstances is the ability to
provide limited access to a service at a reduced price. In situations in
which an organization can simply not afford unlimited access to extremely expensive services (e.g., small libraries and Chemical Abstracts) it should be possible to provide a limited and still annually
budgeted plan. If a library cannot operate with transactional fees due to
unknown annual costs, a simultaneous user limit and/or limited hours
plan might be developed. This is yet another type of customized service
model that can be negotiated in a balance between dollars spent and services offered.

An example of a set of reduced cost access options is offered by the
American Geophysical Union (AGU). In addition to their traditional
site license for journals based upon FTE, they also offer a restricted Per
User plan with a simultaneous seat limitation, and an Annual Access
Fee plan with significantly reduced prices for little-used materials.

In another example, Wiley offers a Basic Access model which is free
with print journals; this plan has simultaneous user limitations and provides no usage statistics. Wiley also offers an alternative electronic
journal option based upon 80% of the existing journal base price which
offers unlimited access to 80% of an organizations used titles, with an
additional 10% fee designated for limited credits to the remaining titles
(or subsets). In this scenario there is an immediate 10% savings, but
there is also no cap on transactional use, and organizations might over-
run their credit amount.

There are many plans being proposed, and many options for organizations to evaluate and negotiate. This many customized pricing approaches cannot practically exist as thousands of deals between vendors
and individual organizations. What is required is a profile approach
based upon a small number of standard packages. Package profiles
would be developed for library groups using research level, potential
user population, and service options as criteria.

NEW PARADIGM MODELS

Let us now explore the changing service options and the associated
fee structures that might be put in place. Delivery capabilities for online
materials have produced completely new options such as added-value
online materials, unbundled materials, and simultaneous user limits.

However, the cost models that accompany the present services are still based upon traditional approaches such as subscriptions and book-based loan periods. Existing cost models do not accurately reflect the real possibilities. What is needed is a new cost paradigm that includes a variety of options based upon system possibilities and user preferences.

The existing delivery and cost models persist in presenting paper-based delivery options with only a few exceptions. While a few radically different models exist–such as the BioMed Central "institutional" page charge option and a few author subsidized journal models (e.g., Optics Express), most online journal subscriptions are relatively unchanged. Journal material may be unbundled at the article level in terms of the release date and page numbers, but packaging is still based upon the concept of a traditional journal. Publishers have not endorsed sales of journal materials at the article level; this type of sub-journal access is still restricted to transactional models. Of course there are a few free online journals, many sponsored and hosted by societies (e.g., the American Physical Society's PRST-AB). The long-term revenue stream to support the infrastructure has yet to be determined for many of these early adopters, and some have even returned to paper-based subscriptions for the short-term. Book sales and book standing orders continue to be based upon traditional models as well. New options for books should include searching across online materials and providing unbundled access to chapters or even subunits (images, charts, etc.).

These new online discovery and delivery mechanisms can provide more flexible and customized services and the capabilities of these systems should drive the development of new payment schema. The integration of the many isolated online services (i.e., journal indexes, online journals, online reference works, and online book series) are based upon new tools and standards; the utilization of XML descriptions and various metadata definitions of materials will result in these new unbundled products. What types of cost models will be required and/or possible based upon these new options?

Alternative Journal Cost Model Options

Another important step in the re-analysis of the current electronic journal commercial distribution model is to reconsider the traditional journal subscription as the only means of subsidizing the distribution of all peer reviewed materials. In the current climate, subscriptions provide publishers with guaranteed revenues when producing packages of material regardless of the commercial value of the actual items in the package. Given our new ability to track usage and provide on-demand delivery, we should be able to develop some alternative delivery and charging algorithms.

As we unbundle and/or monitor the use of items within traditional subscription packages, we have a financial responsibility to modify our existing collection profiles, aiming toward more accountable charging methodologies. After we have identified our local use patterns, we should be able to migrate our Big Deal package plans to a blend of traditional and alternative charging approaches. We can supplement traditional subscriptions for highly used journal materials with tiered plans for lesser-used materials that provide various levels of annual payments based upon use (Stern, 1999). We may also include various types of transactional (pay-per-view) access, with allocation plans for both annual credits covering materials within predetermined packages and one-time purchases. The annual credit accounts will offer for the type of library budgeting required in order to provide pressure-free end user access.

A modification and enhancement to this PPV approach is to create arrangements with publishers to provide seamless access to portions of their materials through a third party vendor in order to track usage and determine fair pricing for future years. This model may also allow for relief from double-payment of Copyright Clearance Center charges for legal "fair use" materials.

An Example Transactional Agent Model

The author is working with the Infotrieve information supplier to develop a Balanced Access Model in which a variety of transactional delivery models are available. In this early stage, the library would make arrangements with individual publishers, but this may become more centralized over time. The Delivery Agent would be responsible for tracking usage, validation, and annual reporting in order to revise these plans annually. Imagine packages (or individual titles) at somewhat reduced subscription costs that guarantee a level of access . . . with annual reviews of use statistics to determine if these titles should be migrated to the higher cost unlimited plans (or dropped to purely transactional approaches). This model is seen as a solution to a variety of problematic situations.

First, it offers a Differential Pricing Model for items previously available from Big Deal plans, particularly for those materials that based upon use data no longer deserve traditional subscriptions. As we break the Big Deal plans over the next few years, or at least reduce the selected core and supplementary titles included, we need new models for access to some of these now unbundled materials that provide some guaranteed support (revenue) and seamless access.

Now imagine that a publisher does not want to deal with the complexities of these multi-level subscription validation issues. In our scenario, the publisher and the library determine a fair price based upon use data, and the publisher then sends a message to Infotrieve granting permission to deliver online titles for a predetermined delivery cost . . . no Copyright Clearance Center fee would be involved. This plan provides seamless access for less sophisticated publishers and also provides a level of guaranteed revenue to the publisher based upon quality/use. Large publishers and aggregators may well be able to handle these complexities and not need the third party portion in order to implement these types of reduced unbundled access plans.

This plan would also allow libraries to use this same delivery method to receive online copies of materials that are now available only in paper format (whether the paper is cancelled or this instituted as an add-on product).

By now it is obvious that while there is added-value to the Big Deal approach, under tight budgetary circumstances, transactional access does provide adequate service for many types of materials. The early Louisiana State University cancellation test, implemented before many of the newer online document delivery options even existed, certainly showed that this on-demand delivery option can identify funds for reallocation with little significant impact on research and teaching. One even wonders why libraries immediately paid the additional costs for online versions of many infrequently used journals? One also wonders how to really measure the impact of cancellations. Even though we now have better use statistics, can we actually find a casual relationship between access to the larger domain and the quality of research?

In the long run, we must decide if we choose to continue to support short-term access to a long-term economically non-viable peer review and journal delivery model or if we migrate toward long-term access to a customized core collection of unbundled research materials with seamless transactional access to specific outlying requests.

Example Alternative Journal Distribution Approaches

There are more radical alternatives being developed without the complete range of traditional commercial underpinning. Many of these are society and university collaborations providing both less expensive distribution plus scholar enhancements.

An interesting alternative is the combination of alternative peer review and revenue sources provided by BioMed Central. Their Faculty of 1000 <http://www.facultyof1000.com/browse/> provides a "virtual review" peer review overlay, and their open access BioMed Central journal collection <http://www.biomedcentral.com/> offers an institutional member pricing model that waives the need for each author to pay a $500 processing fee per manuscript.

An example of a very alternative model which removes peer review is the DSPACE repository located at MIT. Of course it is easier to remove peer review for this system while there is still a parallel peer review network in place for each discipline.

"Some academics argue that the peer-review process handicaps their ability to get timely information into circulation, and DSpace offers an alternative to traditional avenues of access. DSpace also sets as one of its goals the indefinite preservation of data. One researcher from MIT noted that vast amounts of information have already been lost in the digital age, and the DSpace project aims to eliminate such loss. Officials from MIT estimated that the software for DSpace, which is available free online, has been downloaded 3,400 times and that there are around 100 institutions evaluating DSpace as a tool to archive their faculties' research" <http://www.dspace.org/>.

Online Book Options

The slightly modified traditional models used for early online book and standing order access must be redesigned to create scalable and more powerful products. Many of the present models are based upon simultaneous user limits and loan periods as if materials were still paper based. Unlike one-time paper purchasing, online books have annual fees for every year you provide access to a title, and the algorithms used across publishers and aggregators offer a variety of options with little regard to real library budgets and capabilities. Many systems also require annual reviews of every title, which should be an option, but should not be the only way to review materials within packages. Other packages provide no choice in what materials are included within a package. Obviously a balance of these options needs to be developed for tailoring services to local needs.

In terms of enhancements, at a minimum, these systems should provide unbundled access to chapters or even subunits (images, charts, etc.). At the larger level, these search and delivery systems should search across stand-alone books and materials within book series. One could also imagine using agent profiles to search across publishers.

Charging methods for book materials could include the following types of options:

1. One-Time Book Purchases

These could be static purchases with a set time period. There may be no updating of materials (if this is possible, using archival editions). Perhaps there would be no added-value links to outside materials. These one-time purchases could be ordered after individual selector analysis or through pre-created packages–organized by agents across publishers or by discipline.

2. Annual Fee

Standing orders for an online book could be handled with an annual maintenance fee. The annual fee would be determined over time based upon use statistics within standard categories. There would be one annual block fee for all items receiving less than a threshold number of uses per year. These materials could be ordered and tracked by title, or by a group of titles within a discipline–through arrangements with individual selectors and publishers or across publishers. This discipline-based approach requires analysis, and for economies of scale this might best be accomplished using profiles-across consortia of librarians or through agents.

3. Series

There are two options for these materials: create a standing order for all volumes in a series or treat each volume as an individual monograph. Series could be charged on a simple subscription or volumes within a series could be charged a differential price based upon annual use data. If treated as individual monographs, the options are the same as in (1) and (2) above. Searches should be run across all years and materials, with the option of limiting results to items of ownership and/or being notified of document delivery options for non-subscribed portions/chapters.

4. Reference Books

In addition to obtaining items using options (1) or (2) above, an additional option should allow for unbundled access to parts of books: chapters, images, charts, data, links to supplemental material, and online alternative media such as sound bytes, interactive demos, and tutorials. This last option will require detailed XML markup to identify sub-items and novel pricing models for seamlessly or transactionally accessing these sub-units of material.

5. Text Books

In addition to obtaining items using options (1), (2), or (3), these materials could allow for premium access to additional supplementary material such as online testing applications.

Regardless of which methods of accessing online books are selected, it is important to note that both a new annual maintenance charge and inflation on these continuing fees will result in an even larger percentage of budgets being committed at the beginning of each year. This will further skew the balance toward continuations and reduce the flexibility and resources available for one-time purchases.

PROFILES BY AGENTS

The key element to the creation of alternative and flexible search and delivery options is the ability to coordinate and concentrate the many possible plans into a reasonable number of services for practical implementation. While librarians acting in consortia may be able to develop standard profiles, it is more likely that successful and powerful models will be developed through the leverage available by agents acting for a common purpose. The cost of the overhead to an agent will be recovered easily by the lower costs and better plans they can develop utilizing the power and influence they will exert in making deals across publishers. There will need to be a few new players in the field, but perhaps existing players will redesign their services to remain viable. For instance, perhaps the current journal subscription agents will become license experts and the existing document delivery services will also handle the required validation and tracking services for unbundled materials. The tools and possibilities now exist, what is needed is the creativity and initiative to develop profiles and cost models to provide these options in a seamless way when appropriate.

REFERENCE

Stern, David (1999). "Pricing Models: Past, Present, and Future?" *Serials Librarian* 36 (1/2): 301-319.

Incentives for Deconstruction
of the E-Journal

Daniel E. Cleary

SUMMARY. Simply an idea for systematic incentives at all institutional levels necessary to implement institutional archiving of peer-reviewed papers produced by their faculty. Some of the key concerns are addressed outlining the roles of senior faculty, junior faculty, librarians and others in fulfilling what should be an administrative imperative in all academic disciplines and campuses. These concerns include incentives for long term electronic archiving, institutional maintenance of copyright for their employee's intellectual product, motivation of authors to participate in a new publishing paradigm, precise and timely access to peer-reviewed literature and the peer review process. Concludes with a rhetorical calling to arms of all University administrators who would need to lead an assault on an entrenched and well-funded publishing industry. *[Article copies available for a fee from The Haworth Document Delivery Service: 1-800-HAWORTH. E-mail address: <docdelivery@haworthpress.com> Website: <http://www.HaworthPress.com> © 2007 by The Haworth Press, Inc. All rights reserved.]*

KEYWORDS. Electronic archiving, electronic journals, peer-reviewed literature

Daniel E. Cleary is former Head of Information and Access Services, Weill Cornell Medical Library.

Address correspondence to: Daniel E. Cleary, c/o Di Su, York College Library, The City University of New York, 94-20 Guy R. Brewer Boulevard, Jamaica, NY 11451.

[Haworth co-indexing entry note]: "Incentives for Deconstruction of the E-Journal." Cleary, Daniel E. Co-published simultaneously in *The Acquisitions Librarian* (The Haworth Information Press, an imprint of The Haworth Press, Inc.) Vol. 19, No. 1/2 (#37/38), 2007, pp. 135-144; and: *Collection Development Issues in the Online Environment* (ed: Di Su) The Haworth Information Press, an imprint of The Haworth Press, Inc., 2007, pp. 135-144. Single or multiple copies of this article are available for a fee from The Haworth Document Delivery Service [1-800-HAWORTH, 9:00 a.m. - 5:00 p.m. (EST). E-mail address: docdelivery@haworthpress.com].

Available online at http://www.haworthpress.com/web/AL
© 2007 by The Haworth Press, Inc. All rights reserved.
doi:10.1300/J101v19n37_11

INTRODUCTION

In the world of electronic distribution of journal articles the concept of journal becomes arbitrary and convenient only in that it serves to comfort tradition bound academics. Universities must take back the knowledge that they produce. They have the computer departments to assure technical support and service. Universities already have the servers and other infrastructure necessary of archiving their faculty's contribution to the knowledge universe. They have the librarians to assure systematic access to archived knowledge. The rules for citing and indexing are already established. Shared thesauri can easily be created by expanding existing, public domain, subject headings. Subject specialized librarians can be charged with the creation of structured abstracts of a post-reviewed draft of the final papers. Universities create the demand for new acquisition of this knowledge through their housing of the interested students and faculty. The demand can easily be met through a hybrid of cooperative standards and market incentives that not only provide an income stream but also a measurable impact of their faculty's publications that are more accurate and verifiable than current citation statistics. Universities are home to the vast majority of the scientists, researchers, and authors who create new knowledge. The promotion and tenure of these individuals can be made more objective based both upon their contribution to the literature and their service to their fields in the role of being peer reviewers and editorial committee participants. In taking back the knowledge that they produce, Universities can save money on subscriptions, paper, storage, and publishing costs superfluous to the dissemination of information. Universities can earn money while maintaining copyright control of the product of their employees as they do for patents. Universities can assure archival records of their product for generations to come while assuring worldwide access to that product in the present. "Just about ten years ago, the first electronic journals appeared. Publishers didn't know how to sell them, so most were free. Librarians didn't know how to handle them, so their take-up was slow. Both scholars and librarians were unconvinced of their reliability, so paper continued to rule. It took a decade, but ejournals have claimed their place. And there is evidence that many librarians are ready to give up paper for good."[1] This quote is from a 2002 discussion that introduces the annual *Library Journal* analyzation of exorbitant inflation in the prices of ejournal and journal subscriptions. Perhaps it is time to speed up the up-take.

PEER REVIEW

"At the most fundamental, philosophical level, the concept of open society is based on the recognition that people act on imperfect knowledge and that no one is in possession of the ultimate truth."[2] The above statement is the definition of our limit. But we are concerned with decreasing the difference between what our shared knowledge consists of and the limit defined above before we act by performing new research or applying the conclusions of research already performed. Perfecting knowledge for the purpose of sharing through accurate communication is the goal of the peer review process that has been created and maintained by cooperative societies and commercial publishers. Peer review necessitates a speedy review by a motivated reviewing committee. The peer committee must have respect for the intellectual freedom of authors. Committee must have respect for author ownership of ideas (experts capable of reviewing manuscripts should not have interests that would allow for plagiarism or even preemptive presentation of the author's ideas). Post publication peer review should lead to links for retractions by authors or convincing proof of false conclusions of archived (published) papers. Removal of papers with false conclusions, even when requested by the author, is an ethical violation against the record of imperfect truth, which has a function in assisting the endeavor of researchers in not repeating the errors of their colleagues.

Reviewers need to be balanced by including both those closely related to the author's specialized field and those of similar academic rigor in other fields. They need to be balanced if evidence is being presented in the author's paper taking issue with an ongoing controversy in their shared field of expertise.

Reviewers of the literature are peers by definition and have an obligation to their disciplines in assuring that an accurate and relevant presentation of research is maintained so that hypothesis building can be based upon the closest possible point of "imperfect knowledge" to " ultimate truth."[3] Academics must review their peer's literature to assure the continuation of a macrocosm of scientific method. Academics, of course, benefit from this process by the timely discovery of the efforts of their peers. Academics do not necessarily need to perform this function under the auspices of traditional journal or ejournal publishers.

Academics must have the wisdom to realize when they are not worthy of being considered a peer in the reviewing process and due to their being human will need as much structured assistance in maintaining this standard of ethical effort as possible. Departmental colleagues and mentors, listed as members of a standing committee, are probably best equipped to determine the proper fit between a particular paper and a qualified reviewer. These associates will also be best located to provide guidance to the reviewers when they are in doubt of their objective ability to adjudicate the findings of distant peers. The mere acceptance of credentials and reputations of institutional relationships by an editor with a list of past reviewers may compare poorly to a restructured dissemination of papers to reviewers through the academic departments of concerned universities.

Committees charged with manuscript distribution should have intimate knowledge of the potential reviewer's subject knowledge and as well as possible the potential reviewer's professional contacts. Reviewers need to be ultimately responsible for avoiding conflict of interest when papers being reviewed are too close to their own research endeavors. Reviewers are also charged with the avoidance of bias in instances of personal or professional relations with any of the co-authors.

Reviewers must meet the highest standards of confidentiality and compartmentalization. This includes the conscience disallowance of having their thinking about the manuscript effect their thinking process when conducting their own research.

Reviewers should document the written judgments about the papers they are assigned and the Committees that selected the reviewer should follow up the reviewer's documentation with a transcribed question and answer session that clarifies concerns before editorial comments are passed back to the author. Neither the Reviewer nor the committee members should ever allow the rational criticism of a paper turn towards the realm of personal attacks.

PROMOTION AND TENURE

Promotion to tenured Associate Professorship is quite often partially based upon the statistical analysis of literature utilization for the candidate's publications and the candidate's service to his/her discipline. Letters of appointment and determined areas for evaluation of tenure candidates can be made to include responsibilities that will assure the success of University controlled distribution of peer-reviewed information within the disciplines as represented by University departments. University departmental promotion committees can be instructed to weight more heavily on those peer-reviewed publications locally archived and that have standardized usage statistics built upon University server access software. This power of the University administration, if applied gently at first but firmly and consistently over time, will far out weigh the traditional methods of determining the importance of publications that include journal title reputation and Institute of Scientific Information citation statistics. The decision where to publish one's papers as a non-tenured Assistant Professor can easily be manipulated by faculty mentors, departmental chairs, and University administrators.

MEASURABLE IMPACT OF FACULTY PUBLICATIONS

COUNTER (Counting Online Usage of Networked Electronic Resources) is a publishing industry supported organization that is well on the way to standardizing the statistics and providing a set of definitions and formats for data that will allow usage tracking down to the article level and other fine tuned units of information exchange. Tracking software and the Excel spreadsheets that it distributes, to the organizations that archive articles and papers produced by their researchers, will allow for compensation. This compensation can be for both the institution and the authors of the articles. This compensation can be on a basis, that is not immediately pay per view but is, nevertheless, based on actual usage and will allow for billing on an agreed schedule. "COUNTER has been developed to provide a single, international, extendible Code of Practice that allows the usage of online information products and services to be measured in a credible, consistent and compatible way. The COUNTER Code of Practice specifies: the data elements to be measured definitions of these data elements; usage report content, format, frequency and methods of delivery; protocols for combining usage reports from direct use and from use via intermediaries."[4] Detailed auditing specifications will be made available by COUNTER, along with a list of approved auditors, during 2003. A major objective for 2004 is to enhance its value by extending it to cover e-books and other content types and by deepening it to provide more granular reports, such as usage of individual articles.

MEETING THE DEMAND

Universities need to assure the smooth distribution of information in support of their role in nurturing knowledge. Once information has been vetted it deserves to be archived on servers controlled by the University's library. The cost of this archiving can slowly replace those budget items that consists of subsidizing commercial publishers who wish to dominate our 'fair usage' clause with pay per view and denial of Interlibrary Loan (ILL) rights in e-journal contracts. If libraries control the access to copyrighted material produced by the University then ILL agreements of free or subsidized interactions can continue unhampered in the electronic future. Schools deemed worthy of discounted prices could be selected and accounted for in the overall budget. Institutions in heavy need of publications but not in need of fiscal resources can be used as sources to balance library budgets. Institutions who have consistent high usage on both the supply and demand side can be maintained as free sharing partners to simplify accounting procedures and increase the cooperative spirit amongst peer institutions.

Public Service Librarianship is already set up to assure that any secondary searching tools are utilized to their maximum potential for accessing the best information from all open sources. The public service side of the profession has been traditionally isolated from fiscal concerns, and in the vast majority of participants maintains a level of ethical behavior that will assure the proper compensation and fair utilization of information from all providers. In many cases Google will soon be searching our catalogs, thanks to the efforts of OCLC. The indexing tools that now search computer supplied citations from publishers will have no problem adjusting to librarian-standardized citations and tracings for unbundled articles on University servers. These indexing tools already place buttons to URLs of the full-text articles that a library already has rights to and will have no problem utilizing the permanent URLs maintained by the various libraries that make up their customer base. Libraries can either budget for their usage of articles from other institutions or can pass on their costs to their end users through a variety of methodologies that most libraries have already instituted. These methodologies include an expansion of computerized printing accounts, the utilization of manually controlled fine functions on their clientele's circulation records or cash collection at the circulation desk. Those Universities that in the aggregate produce the most used information and will, of course, enjoy a financial advantage as they do when their control of important patents is licensed out to commercial ventures.

SYSTEMATIC ACCESS

Shared thesauri maintained by librarians who are closest to their specialized colleagues who can contribute accurate and timely tracings to their literature are the key to systematic access. Cataloging, a long neglected art in the world of mass distributed monographs and shared MARC records, can become robust with the tools at hand and the task of assuring a proper overlay of bibliographic control for the article holdings of University servers. The assignment of agreed upon subject headings for these electronic items and the strict adherence to cataloging standards will assure present and future ease of access for all. Authority control for personal names and corporate names will be maintained by the author's institutional cataloging librarians with links to agreed upon biographical and contact information. An expanded function of acting as final editor or writers of structured abstracts will assure accurate search results and provide an effective tool for adjudicating usefulness by the end user. The author, an assigned member of the reviewing committee, or the librarian can be utilized for the very important task of writing an objective and accurate abstract. Electronically supplied abstracts from the publishers have proven to be inconsistent in their quality and even in their existence in most databases. The discipline of Librarianship will help to professionalize this role just as it will assure fairness in the delivery process of information distribution.

COMPUTER DEPARTMENTS

In the institutional computer department's control of intranets, networks, firewalls, printers, workstations, departmental Web pages, and campus-wide software including Virtual Private Networking (VPN) access have learned to deal with the annoyance of libraries as consumers and distributors of information. Expanding that tolerance to allowing for the University to complete the act of producers of information through the channel of the library is not beyond their capability of meeting our expectations. Through departmental servers computer departments can also be ready to serve the needs of archiving and distributing non-reviewed literature either in the process of becoming vetted or in the form of data sets and other pre-publication formats. As articles pass peer review they may be transferred to the more accessible servers controlled by the library. To the degree found appropriate by University departments, whose members are the original authors, the servers containing non-reviewed literature, data sets, teaching materials, conference presentations and gray literature can be made available to a wider research audience. Interoperability to allow accessibility to search engines and the maintenance of metadata tagging should be at a minimum standard for assuring the sharing of appropriate resources.

UNIVERSITIES MUST TAKE BACK THE KNOWLEDGE

"As producers of primary research, it is only to be expected that academic institutions would take an interest in capturing and preserving the intellectual output of their faculty, students, and staff. Traditionally, scholarly publishers (as aggregators and distributors) and institutional libraries (as managers and preservers) served complementary roles in facilitating scholarly communication and preserving–albeit in a diffuse and indirect manner–an institution's intellectual legacy. Over the past several decades, however, the economic, market, and technological foundations that sustained this symbiotic publisher-library market relationship have begun to shift."[5]

This symbiotic relationship is dysfunctional at best and if University administrators look at the budget lines for both paper and ejournal serials they will see clearly the enabling role their librarians have been forced into by publishers who print money from the efforts of University faculty. Retaining copyrights of their employee's efforts, as institutions do already for patents, would allow for a great savings in library acquisition budgets after an initial phase of cooperative implementation. Institution held copyrights also has the potential of generating income from outside users of peer-reviewed publications while actually making access to this information cheaper for the end user at outside libraries. The incentive is there and the organizational structure to support institutional archiving is there, as well as the technology. Implementation must come from the top down with a clear understanding of goals, objectives, and timetables. The most important tool of implementation is the appropriate delegation of specific objectives to cooperating bodies of professional organizations that key institutional players participate through their faculty. University Deans and Presidents must agree on strategy, including the commitment of start up capital. Library associations, academic computing associations, and professional organizations need to be charged with specific tasks that are not seen as contradicting any major functions of the organization (such as their being a publisher). Department heads and faculty councils must be charged with generating policies that not only promote open access publishing but also demand it from their junior faculty.

TO COMFORT TRADITION BOUND ACADEMICS

A revolution of this nature should be implemented consistently on as many campuses as possible in a very short period of time so that equitable treatment avoids draining of faculty to Universities that do not adhere to what at first may seem as arbitrary interference with scholarly speech. Senior faculty should be encouraged to participate by submitting their papers to the same process but without formal encouragement. Junior faculty should be shown the advantages through statistical reports on the usage of their publications on a regular basis as compared to average usage through traditional press where available. They should also be made aware that due to shrinking material budgets as compared to astronomical journal price inflation their publications in many journal titles are not being made available to a wide audience despite comprehensive indexing by large databases. All faculty members who publish to institutional servers should receive a share of an access income generated by their writings even though the institution would maintain copyright control. Statewide University systems should cooperate quickly on setting up discipline defined cooperative committees for reviewing one another's submissions in the peer review process. Librarians should set up subject specialized current awareness searches that run automatically and deliver to the desktops of their colleagues the equivalent of annotated table of contents leaving the scouring of table of contents services and home pages of ejournals to those with time to spare.

Universities do not have money to spare, and then comforting their academics is worthy of their concern during a period of transition to an institutional archived environment with incentives. If this transition is to be successful it must come from the top down with an agreed upon plan and a willingness to invest into the hardware and necessary personnel to accommodate the acceptance of duties performed by publishers in the past. Large Universities with in-house presses should have little problem expanding the role of their librarians, computer services personnel and publishing professionals to quickly take on the new functions of institutional review and archiving of faculty publications.

REFERENCES

1. Van Orsdel, L.; Born, K. "Periodicals Price Survey 2002: Doing the Digital Flip." *Library Journal* 127 (April 15, 2002): 51-6.

2. OPEN SOCIETY INSTITUTE-Budapest, The Concept of Open Society. Available: <http://www.osi.hu/>.

3. Ibid.

4. COUNTER, About COUNTER. Available: <http://www.projectcounter.org/about.html>.

5. Crow, R.. The Case for Institutional Repositories: A SPARC Position Paper. Available: <http://www.arl.org/sparc/IR/ir.html>.

PDA Serials:
Practical and Policy Issues for Librarians

Stephen Good

SUMMARY. Personal Digital Assistant serials are not just a subset of electronic serials from an acquisitions/collection development point of view because of their total dependence on patron-owned technology. Even if viewed as a "free" resource there are issues of expense and effort involved in gathering, classifying, and providing access and awareness of what the library has. PDA serials make sense if there is an institutional mandate, a desire for the library to be "cutting edge," or a group of people willing to champion the concept. Otherwise, a library should feel confident waiting until the technology becomes more stable, standardized, and ubiquitous. *[Article copies available for a fee from The Haworth Document Delivery Service: 1-800-HAWORTH. E-mail address: <docdelivery@haworthpress.com> Website: <http://www.HaworthPress.com> © 2007 by The Haworth Press, Inc. All rights reserved.]*

KEYWORDS. Acquisition decisions, electronic resources, innovative collection management, PDA, personal digital assistant, serials

Stephen Good is former Reference and Instructional Librarian, Texas Tech School of Law Library.

Address correspondence to: Stephen Good, 4402 14th Street, Lubbock, TX 79409-0004.

[Haworth co-indexing entry note]: "PDA Serials: Practical and Policy Issues for Librarians." Good, Stephen. Co-published simultaneously in *The Acquisitions Librarian* (The Haworth Information Press, an imprint of The Haworth Press, Inc.) Vol. 19, No. 1/2 (#37/38), 2007, pp. 145-160; and: *Collection Development Issues in the Online Environment* (ed: Di Su) The Haworth Information Press, an imprint of The Haworth Press, Inc., 2007, pp. 145-160. Single or multiple copies of this article are available for a fee from The Haworth Document Delivery Service [1-800-HAWORTH, 9:00 a.m. - 5:00 p.m. (EST). E-mail address: docdelivery@haworthpress.com].

INTRODUCTION

A library may want to appear to be on the "cutting edge" of collection development by offering patrons' collections of PDA serials (electronic serials either customized or created specifically for handheld technology), and the decision may seem easy because PDA serials take up no physical space and may be free to acquire. However, PDA serials require a thorough knowledge of patrons (both in terms of owning PDAs and knowing how to use them) as well as a dynamic conversation between public services, technical services, administrators, and the IT department. Like a four-legged table, all four areas of the library must be "with the program" for a PDA serials campaign to succeed–gathering the resources, promoting their availability, helping patrons with inevitable problems and adjustment and being allowed the staff time and energy to make the acquisitions work.[1]

EVERY INNOVATION WILL NOT INEVITABLY END UP IN LIBRARIES

In the last three years I have made extensive use of three public libraries in Oxnard, California; Kingston, Ontario (Canada); and Lubbock, Texas. I loved all three libraries' systems and I have developed a special place in my heart for branch libraries, but that is not why I mention them. What I was interested in was what multimedia materials I could check out. Oxnard was the hands down winner with lots of movies, books on tape and music on CD-ROM. Oxnard even had computer software which I found both impressive and unusual for a public library. Kingston had books-on-tape and CD-ROM, some very good book-tape kits for children and an excellent classical music collection (you could actually buy the vinyl LP version and check out the CD-ROM version of the same Bach concerto at the same time if you wanted to). Kingston pulled their small children's computer software for copyright reasons and their popular music collection was nowhere near as impressive as their classical music. Lubbock has movies on DVD and VHS, talking books on CD-ROM (more so than on tape) and has no music in any format or genre. The mayor of Oxnard had a strong education background and was a strong supporter of the library. The Kingston public library is very old and traces its roots to a Mechanics Institute and the music CDs are replacing a strong vinyl music collection (the one that was being sold off) which in turn springs from the Mechanics Institution education/cultivation model. Lubbock is not as well funded as either of the other two and is adopting a "one thing at a time policy"–building up the audio books and movie collections before getting to the music. And as everyone knows, patrons are far more likely to steal music than anything else so the best policy is to display the cases and store the actual discs or tapes which raises storage issues.

All these comments are based on personal observation by a dad with three (soon four) kids who checks out materials by the linear foot rather than on any carefully planned, consultant-prepared reading list. The point is simply that libraries are different based on their history, their funding, their physical setup and their inclination. Music can be used as a way to lure library-shy users into the facility (Oxnard) or as an expression of culture and sophistication in a smallish town with a large university and pride in its symphony orchestra (Kingston) or as an item which is still a few boxes down on the checklist (Lubbock).

All that in order to say this: the first thing we have to consider about electronic documents is that no matter how the e-book industry and electronic document format flourishes (which itself is not guaranteed) libraries will not embrace the new medium with equal enthusiasm or budget allocations. To think otherwise would be as absurd as expecting all libraries everywhere regardless of size and type to have copies of *Charlotte's Web*, *The Complete Works of William Makepeace Thackeray*, *A Medical Practitioner's Guide to SARS* and *Product Liability Cases: The Year in Review*.

HYBRID NATURE OF PDA AND PDA SERIALS

A library's decision with regards to acquiring electronic serials for PDA revolves around the hybrid nature of PDA serials as a medium. Unlike the self-sufficiency of books or the widespread availability of CD- and DVD-players, the first problem a librarian faces is knowing how many, if any, of his/her patrons even own PDAs. And as PDAs become incorporated into multi-functional cell phone/digital cameras, the wider availability of "standard option" PDAs included in these devices will not automatically mean that every PDA-owner is a PDA-user. And it would be a rare, and wealthy, library which could afford to purchase PDAs for every patron yet having a handful of PDAs to loan out at the circulation desk may not justify an intensive PDA-serial project. Conversely, there may be libraries which will find themselves part of a larger institution-wide PDA-initiative where all the doctors, lawyers, salespeople, or administrators that the library serves are provided with PDAs and expected to use them, and the librarian would be expected to contribute to the success of the initiative by bringing all the PDA content possible into play. For now, it is probably safe to say that libraries which exist within the "time is money" paradigm are more likely to explore PDA serials than libraries where patrons use their PDAs to play Whack-a-mole with (the little stick thing that comes in a PDA).

PDA SERIALS ACQUISITION WILL REMAIN OPTIONAL FOR MOST LIBRARIES

Apart from the abovementioned institutional PDA initiatives, most libraries will probably not find themselves compelled to even provide access to any PDA materials, serial or otherwise. Like PC software or classical music on Digital Audio Tape, PDA materials will remain optional for most libraries. Given the variety of proprietary formats, PDA content may suffer the same fate as electronic books and readers: a compelling theoretical success rate with a perpetual brink-of-bankruptcy real world track record. Part of the problem is definitional. "PDA serial" is a term like "virtual library" or "computer application" rather than "Microsoft Word document" or "Braille book with audiotape."

Another interesting characteristic of mobile documents is that even though they are invisible and intangible does not mean that they are software-independent. They are not all ASCII files floating around ready to download into any device which we care to use. Some are proprietary, some are dated, some are their own special form of software for which devices and operating systems no longer exist and some are trapped behind websites which have gone out of date or otherwise become a locked room in cyberspace. Mobile documents, whether they are "out there" or "in here" whether they are owned or leased still require maintenance. It is one thing to move a one-page document from Word to WordPerfect, but when you are talking hundreds and thousands and especially hundreds of thousands of documents that becomes a chore in itself. At about this point in the process, someone is bound to ask, "Excuse me, why exactly are we doing this again?"

To the extent that anything on a computer can, in theory, be "synchronized" (imported from/exported to) a PDA, then to the extent that electronic serials persevere, PDA serials will endure as well. Since a library could do up a customized PDA "News from the Library" serial, a

library could guarantee that there was a PDA serials program in existence until there was conclusive evidence that no one was downloading
the News serials for months on end.

EVEN IF NOT A FAD, PDAs MAY BE LEFT TO PATRONS ON THEIR OWN

Even if there are clear indications of heavy patron use of PDA materials, a library may still consciously choose to take no steps in this direction whatsoever. The fact that every patron in a library uses a cell phone
does not mean that the library has to provide a database of download-
able ringtones. The librarians may decide that like music files or
multi-player online games, PDA serials are another area where patron
enthusiasm and not librarian professionalism is the dominant criterion.

PDA serials are high-maintenance and ephemeral which account
both for their popularity and usefulness but also unnecessary headache
and effort in libraries where they are not in demand. The librarians will
have to decide if acquiring and/or organizing PDA serials would be an
extension of, or a distraction from, the library's core mission. As with
electronic serials, there could also be major challenges or issues which
arise almost overnight. Currently, PDAs are "under the radar." But if
PDA downloading of serials and other documents became common,
there could be licensing issues which arose and "expiration" software
demanded by suppliers so that information cannot be permanently
moved from the library's computers to the patrons' hard drives. A
PDA's mobility means that electronic site licenses no longer apply because the locus of control over content has shifted from library to patron.

A further relationship between electronic serials and PDAs is that
those libraries which experience heavy demand and use of electronic serials will be more likely to receive requests for PDA serials than libraries where electronic serials are unknown or under-used. PDA serial
usage is not just a matter of the availability of the technology and the
content; there is also a need for the patrons to be technologically
"savvy" enough to access the content. Libraries will need to supply a
certain level of expertise but "spoon feeding" (providing extensive
PDA assistance to those who can't master the technology) even a small
number of patrons would be close to impossible.

PDAs ARE A MEDIUM RATHER THAN A FORMAT

PDAs are a medium rather than a format. So while we can talk about what books or CDs or DVDs are "in print," we cannot as easily talk about what PDA serials are available. Any electronic document or resource can potentially be PDA-friendly, so to speak, dictated only by the memory of the particular device in question. Given the size of the screen and the typical use to which PDAs are put, however, a PDA is more suited to headline news and short paragraphs than to 75-page academic articles with extensive footnoting. Newspapers, magazines, and even websites which create versions of themselves intended for PDA use will often dumb down and/or digest the content of the original, and sometimes what is left is so fleeting as to be of little use other than to serve as an advertisement for the real thing.

PDAs are intended for checking e-mail, making appointments, and writing short notes. Likewise, the content which is best suited for them also tends to be short: factoids, ready reference, news items, etc. You can put a novel into a PDA but the fact that one printed page will now amount to 5+ screens may dampen your enthusiasm.

PDAs HAVE ALLURE, BUT "IF IN DOUBT, WAIT"

The allure of PDA serials for a library is compelling–they are trendy, technical, talked-about and in some cases, free. Like public domain e-books, PDA serials would seem to be a good feature to add to a library's portal. The flip side is that to succeed in offering PDA resources you have to know your patrons well, know the PDA-technology well, know your ILS/OPAC well, and have clear policies in place which let the patron know what can and cannot be done. Offering PDA support is not something to do when you are migrating from one library software system to another. Offering PDA resources is not something to do if no librarians or staff own or use PDAs themselves. PDAs are a minefield of proprietary technology–whereas librarians may feel comfortable with Microsoft Word and Internet Explorer/Netscape, the kinds of questions you will have to field with PDAs will be all over the map. This is dictated by the nature of PDAs as a dependent technology–you can use a PDA as a standalone but they are intended as the mobile/updateable extension of a desktop or laptop computer. For a library to provide direct-to-PDA resources would necessitate not only having "docking stations" but having docking stations for the various and sundry technologies available.

As with computers, the best advice is "if in doubt, wait." Realistically, a library needs at least two specific people to consider offering PDA serials–a project champion and a technical guru. Offering PDA serials is as far from going out and purchasing the books to create a mystery novel leisure reading section as possible. With books, other people will do the work for you; with PDAs, the library will have to do a lot of work internally. Patrons will come with downloading problems, with "why can't I see this map image?" problems, with questions around why certain PDA resources are free and accessible and others are password and/or subscription protected.

In the same way that PDAs are a hybrid form of technology, neither totally in the library's control nor totally in the patron's control, PDA serials are a hybrid format. A library will purchase books and let patrons borrow them. Libraries may also cover the cost of ILL materials which are given or lent to patrons. Say, for argument's sake that a library rents a copy of a book which is only borrowed by one patron before being sent back–does the fact that the book could have been lent to other people during the rental period mean that the rental cost is amortized over all those potential borrowings? By contrast, if a library patron requests a copy of a book or article which is available in electronic form and which would be given (and given only) to that one patron, is that a violation of the "potential borrowing" protocol? What if that scenario is modified again and the library pays for a download license for a PDA serial but the actual downloaded products contain expiration software which will make the serial or collection of articles vanish after a one week or one month period? Even though the PDA resource is still being given away, has it now come back under a library protocol umbrella?

SCENARIO:
THE LIBRARY AND THE FREE PDA SERIALS

To simplify the discussion for now, let us consider PDA serials which are free. They may only be an abridged or digested version of a larger resource, but let us assume that the library patrons can get access to some content for free. Let's further assume that PDA document standards are in place so that downloading and reading problems are manageable. And of course there is both demand and content which will satisfy that demand. How would a library proceed?

The reason to consider such an idealized scenario is that even when most of the obstacles are removed, there are still PDA serial acquisition issues which remain. As with government documents, brochures, donated books, and vertical file materials, a library can obtain free resources and still have to think twice about accepting them or how to process them. Even with PDA serials which take up no physical space in the library (a computer disk which is half-full takes up the same amount of physical space as one is which is 100% full) and are no burden on the acquisitions budget, there are still issues.

The seeming benefits of this PDA scenario–a free resource that takes up no physical space–are offset by the fact that until some time and effort is devoted to drawing attention to the PDA materials, they are invisible . . . At our library we have 3,000 full-text electronic books, but I can never remember where they are. Occasionally you bump into them in a catalog record but since they are a fairly specialized collection you are more likely to want to browse the e-book collection–but to get there involves burrowing through several layers of the OPAC. And, since we only have one (borrowable) copy of each of the 3,000 books, there isn't much incentive to bring the collection forward because everyone would want the same books and you can only have them for 24-48 hours anyway. And currently we aren't set up so that you can "borrow" them onto a mobile device and they display very awkwardly on the computer screen. If we had money to upgrade, where would the best place be to spend it–more copies per title, borrowing privileges, dedicated readers with larger screens, more PR, more omnipresent representation in the OPAC? With mobile documents libraries are re-learning what they discovered with government documents, pamphlets, and Reader's Digest condensed books–just because materials are free and plentiful does not mean they do not have costs associated with them. Ironically, the very "invisibility" of mobile documents is offset by the cost of having to create visibility for them. It's as though each mobile document has to have a book dummy created for it, catalogued, labeled, and put on the shelf. "This book also available as an e-document." Would patrons appreciate a sticker like that on the actual book? While they remain invisible, they will not be used at all. As soon as the library starts drawing attention to them, money and labor hours become an issue. Whether the resources are catalogued or put on a library portal there are immediately maintenance and classification issues which arise. PDA products have demonstrated the same level of volatility as websites in terms of being "here today and gone tomorrow." Electronic serials may have more expense and more complex licensing issues involved, but they are an evolution of print journals and therefore have more staying power over the long term.

PDAs INDICATIVE OF BLURRING OF DISTINCTIONS WITHIN LIBRARY ACQUISITIONS

To look at this aspect of mobile documents, we need to consider the library catalog. The library catalog stands in relation to the resources of the library in the same way that an index stands in relation to the contents of a book–as a finder's aid, as a simplified outline of the material to which it points. The library or book is big, the index or catalog is smaller and more manageable. The index or catalog also imposes an order and hierarchy–alphabetical, numerical, or conceptual–which is superimposed on the collection or text. Nothing controversial so far. Where the controversy comes in is that at some point in the not to distant future computer power and computer memory will be such that we will no longer have a library catalog we will have a library/catalog. In other words, the library's catalog and the library's resources will be coextensive. Now of course this will not be THE library/catalog, this will be A library/catalog but there will be a catalog which will have call numbers and subject headings but also the full text for thousands if not millions of items. In one sense we are already there because library patrons can readily have an "out of library" experience which includes access to many if not all the library's full-text databases. The same technology that is going to put video stores out of business–the ability to download full-length, feature films onto a recording device in the home but which will prevent copying and will have an auto-destruct, time-out feature, will allow libraries to do the same thing with library materials. Library patrons will have thousands if not millions of documents which are right there on their computer with the only catch that they constantly need to be "renewed" by establishing a connection with the home library. The first offshoot of this is that the computer power at the library end will also have expanded exponentially and libraries will have a "use driven" acquisitions budget which may have the obtaining of new journals and mobile documents resembling the stock market exchange more than any notion of purchasing books from a warehouse. Of course there will still be print materials being acquired and librarians will need to study these "use maps" to see what materials patrons are completely overlooking–rather than "weeding" what does not circulate, the librarians' job will be to draw attention to those electronic materials which have been acquired but which are being underutilized. And this is why the notion of a library/catalog–where the holdings and the description of those holding converge and collapse into one another–is so interesting. In this library/catalog environment, the different departments and aspects of the library will not exist in a horizontal, factory-like relationship to each other where orders are placed, materials are obtained, cataloging is done and then material is sent out to the public. Rather, the different aspects of the library will be like transparent sheets placed on top of one another–what is used will be monitored hour by hour and day by day. New acquisitions can be made constantly but also in totally different configurations (a "trial subscription" can be worked through the entire system in a matter of hours with both the appropriate cataloging insertions made and a public announcement to the entire library community) and reference librarians will need to be totally conversant in the inner workings of the library catalog as well as suggesting short-term acquisitions to satisfy individual or small group requests. Of course there will be policy and procedure implications–will the library subscribe to a PDA serial knowing that only one person will make use of that journal? We buy books that no one ever checks out, so there is nothing wrong in theory with this kind of purchase since we know in advance there is a demand for the item, but it may still raise the shackles (wrong cliché) of certain library administrators who do not mind spending money on ILL items but think there is something amiss in catering to a single library patron.

HIDDEN COSTS OF PDA ACQUISITIONS

The money a library "saves" in acquiring a free resource like PDA resources is offset by the advertising and education that the library must invest in alerting patrons to what is available and how these materials are to be accessed. This is why a PDA-mandate and ensuring that going down the PDA path is commensurate with the institution's mission is worthwhile.

Not surprisingly, the solution for both PDA resources and electronic serials is the same–only catalog what you have control over and only acquire what you can control. And you have the option of creating a PDA resource area which is simply a section of the libraries website–thus treating PDA resources like websites rather than electronic serials. The volatility in the e-book area which seems to run roughly parallel to PDA resources suggests that reliance on any kind of PDA resource supplier or aggregator is no guarantee that the resources will be available into the future. PDA resources are as much a faddish gamble as an extension or evolution of other publishing ventures. Whereas if the library creates PDA-friendly versions of existing electronic documents, serial or otherwise, the resource is more stable and the main effort is in translating the documents into PDA accessible files.

Another dynamic which flows from the hybrid nature of PDAs is the confusion created in the patrons' (and possibly the library staff's) minds as to who is responsible for what. If you borrow a book and lose the book, you pay for it. If the book falls apart while you are reading it, you bring this (hopefully) to the library's attention. If a VHS tape or DVD is unplayable, you point this out to someone at the circulation desk upon return. If your VCR or DVD player bursts into flames, you need to get it repaired or buy a new one at your own expense (and hope that there was no library movie in the player at the time). By contrast, if a library starts advertising the availability of PDA content and patrons run into problems they will expect assistance from the library. Not with the PDA device itself, but with any operating problems they may have while they learn how to master it. This is the problem posed by "the digest is free, the full version costs money"–patrons may see the library as denying rather than providing access to what they want. In the same way the libraries are now expected to provide access to the Internet by having computers in the library, a library should anticipate that launching a PDA resource campaign may bring forward patrons who expect the library to loan out PDAs so that they can access the materials.

If the key to even pursuing a PDA extension of the library's holdings is to have a project champion and a technical guru, success also requires making a thorough survey of staff and patrons enthusiasm. A library wouldn't be likely to buy books written in Serbian if no one on staff or among the patrons read the language. Likewise, there is little reason to harvest PDA resources if there is no interest in them. As mentioned above, PDA ownership is not the same as PDA expertise (or even usage). There is also a counterintuitive aspect of PDAs–not everyone that you think would have one does nor does everyone who owns them use them as extensively as you might expect. Personally, I was surprised to notice that of all the publishers' sales representatives that came to visit me, none of them used PDAs. This seemed very odd but the explanation was quick in coming–the reps had elaborate paper systems which they had used for a long time and they were reluctant to shift over to another system which might or might not map 1:1 onto the paper system they relied on. The other is that any survey of staff and patrons needs to be repeated at least once every six months. As libraries have gradually migrated from VHS tape to DVD, likewise, a library may find that as PDA devices become more ubiquitous that their staff and patrons are moving from non-owners to owners and from non-users to users. And in the institutional setting this can happen almost overnight–as we witness colleges and universities which require incoming students to have laptop computers, the PDA profile of the library's community can shift very suddenly. There is a certain "time is money" factor to PDAs–people who have no appointments and receive no e-mail are unlikely to be clamoring to use PDA serials.

REASONS WHY A LIBRARY WOULD ACQUIRE PDA SERIALS

Given the complications, technical and otherwise, what would make a library to decide to pursue the PDA route? Well, as with the abandonment of the card catalog, the prevalence of PDAs and the lowering of the bar could make catering to PDAs easy and failure to do so politically unwise. However, there are less dire reasons for offering PDA resources.

In whatever community the library is, PDA offerings could go a certain way to show that the library is "cutting-edge." PDAs are a natural (even related) extension of digital/e-chat reference and offering wireless access to the library's catalog and resources. Especially with the advent of PDA/cell phone combinations, PDA resources can serve as a kind of library outreach for those patrons who are uninterested in the book collection.

Because PDAs are built around a "permanently updating" model of information access, PDA resources encourage constant, ongoing, interactive and frequent contact with the PDA resource supplier. As with library portals, PDA resources steer the patrons through rather than around or away from the library. True, the trick with turning non-patrons into patrons is that the library has to acclimatize them to the library culture, but better to have to introduce a PDA user to the magazine or journal collection than never to have that opportunity.

And for regular library patrons, the argument is even more compelling because accommodating PDAs can mean that library service is taken up several notches. PDAs are part of a larger dynamic made possible by better software and more computer power put at the disposal of libraries: to offer each patron individualized, customizable, and expansive access to libraries aggregated by the library.

One of the exciting challenges of PDAs is that reward a library for being transparent and for breaking down barriers between the technical and public departments within the library. PDAs and individualized access create the perfect opportunity for libraries to allow patrons to "vote" on what electronic resources a library should acquire. And not just "vote" in the sense of monitoring the usage of electronic resources, but vote in the sense of vote. This does not mean "acquisitions monopolized by the tyrannical PDA minority" it just means that PDAs become the symbol of a new era for the particular library–patrons have more nuanced input into the library acquisitions process rather than just being another name on the waiting list for a forthcoming bestseller.

How can PDAs bring down the barriers within a library? Well, of course all PDAs or anything else can do is to create an opportunity, but the library can certainly fail to grasp or even reject the opportunity. If the library decides to seize the chance, PDAs go from being a technical hybrid to a conceptual and procedural hybrid as well. In the scenario just mentioned, the PDA becomes a public input device which needs to be filtered, processed, and approved before being passed on to the (technical) acquisitions people. Conversely if the library decides to acquire and catalog PDA resources, this technical accomplishment will be invisible and hidden until the public departments–reference and public relations/advertising–of the library draw attention to the new availability of this resource. And the IT people will inevitably be drawn into this process both in recommending what technical protocols the library should go with and with helping individual patrons troubleshoot their PDA devices. In the end, PDA serials are not really a test of how technologically proficient a library is, they are a test of how service-oriented a library is. If there is no call for such a service, then the library is better off to focus on other areas, but if PDAs are already widely accepted by a library's patrons, then offering assistance and resources will definitely make better use of patrons' time and this should translate into closer ties with, greater support for and making more use of the library and its resources.

Which brings us to the bottom-up way of looking at this situation. Something which has always been the case but which is intensified, brought more clearly into focus with mobile documents is just how truly amazing libraries really are in terms of identifying and acquiring information. Because libraries do not have to worry about the profit margin in acquiring an item, they deal with incredibly more vendors and publishers than any bookstore could ever dream of. What the creation of the library/catalog and the collapsing/superimposition of the different library departments is going to mean is that libraries will have the opportunity to connect patrons and vendors in a way that in the past would have been not only unlikely but unheard of. Libraries have never done "special orders" in the sense of using their expertise to obtain books for patrons. A patron can suggest an "addition to the collection" which may entail a great deal of investigative work by the library to actually find the item, but this is still viewed as adding an item to the collection which just happens to satisfy the needs of a specific patron.

The reason why libraries have not ordered books for patrons apart from the fact that bookstores exist to offer this service is partly because the logistics run contrary to how libraries work–if you start "buying" books and then passing the cost on to patrons you end up having to haggle over prices ("this isn't what I thought it would cost"), you are subsidizing their request with staff time, and you end up having to handle money and act as a collection agency which is not how librarians want to spend their time. But what happens in the creation of the library/catalog where the resources and the descriptions are co-extensive is that another layer collapses onto this as well–the publisher/vendor/acquisitions information. "The library subscribes to this journal from volume 15-current, however here is the link if you would like to contact the publisher about earlier issues."

Of course there will be problems. Patrons will wonder why this issue of a journal is something where the library will pick up the tab and why this other journal is something where the patron has to have their credit card handy. But that is not the crucial point. The crucial point is that there will be a transparency in the library's areas of expertise and not only will reference and acquisitions be in closer contact but also library patrons will be able to benefit from that area of library expertise that surpasses what a bookstore is capable of offering.

This is not an unheard of possibility. Diligent library patrons have always been able to borrow *Books in Print* to track down items they wanted to order for themselves. What is new is the seamlessness with which patrons will be able to shift from the library holdings to items they want to purchase for themselves. There will be charges of elitism–that the library is trying to shift the expense of acquisitions onto the patrons. Well, that is no different than all the thousands and millions of books which libraries have not bought which people have wanted to read. Where this will not be a problem is with free materials. It may strike patrons as odd that the library has different categories for "free materials." Why not just "have" everything. The answer of course is that free materials are not free if you have to process them. What will emerge are two categories–those materials, free and paid for, which the library owns and goes to the trouble of cataloging and putting into the library/catalog and that second group of materials for which the library provides access but does not pay for acquisition or upkeep. Even in this second category, the library may add some value by subscribing to a search service which will allow the patrons to search all the electronic depositories and copyright-free full-text websites with a single interface.

None of this is inevitable, but mobile electronic documents will allow the opportunity for libraries to take their light out from under the basket and put it on a lamp stand for all to see.

LIBRARIANSHIP IS A CONVERSATION

Librarianship is a conversation. A consultant who visited our library recently in answering to the "How are we going to overcome these seemingly insurmountable technical and political problems?" said, "Some things are best worked out in quiet tones in a casual conversation." PDA is a perfect example of an issue which needs quiet tones and casual conversation. Any administrator who goes into this with an attitude of "This is going to happen and it's going to happen by Friday or you're all fired!" is courting disaster. At any stage, for any number of reasons the answer to "Should we pursue this PDA thing?" could be "No" or "Not Yet."

What is especially interesting about PDA is how many-sided the conversation is. The people in technical services and IT have to be sufficiently comfortable and up to speed with the library software and computer system that they feel comfortable embarking on what will be a brand new (and possibly steep) learning curve. The people in public services will be the first ones to gauge how much PDA activity and what kind of reception PDA serials accessed through the library catalog would get. The library will be in conversation not only with other libraries but also with publishers and vendors. Libraries may end up convincing publishers to explore PDA pricing and availability for titles they have in electronic form but have not considered launching as a PDA product yet. Most importantly, the librarians and library staff will need to be in conversation with library patrons to see if the whole venture is supported, appreciated, opposed, or a matter of indifference. And all parties are in a conversation with the future of technology which could render PDA irrelevant, omnipresent, or enfolded within a yet-to-be-invented technology.

REFERENCE

1. Stephen Good is former Reference/Instructional Librarian at Texas Tech School of Law Library in Lubbock, Texas. Key ideas for this article were generated in discussions with Sharon Scott and Joseph Blackburn, both librarians in Lubbock as well.

Index

Page numbers followed by f indicate figures, and those marked with t indicate tables.

AALL. *See* American Association of
    Law Libraries (AALL)
ABC-Clio, 102
ABI-Inform, 80
Academic(s), e-materials and, 10-11
Academic libraries
    electronic journal delivery in, 15-45
        communication from publishers,
            35-41
        grace period in, 33-35
        introduction to, 16
        pricing issues related to, 29-33
        publishers or agents for
            subscriptions, 24-29
        troubleshooting in, 22-24
    electronic serials in, 75-82. *See also*
        Electronic serials, in
        academic libraries
    print serials in, 76-77
Academic Search Elite (EBSCO), 4-5,
    15,20,80,100,101,103,104
Access Activation Code, 26
Acrobat Capture 3.0, 114,115
Across the Board, 108
Adobe Acrobat, 114
Agents, for online subscriptions, 24-29
AGU. *See* American Geophysical
    Union (AGU)
ALA. *See* American Library
    Association (ALA)
American Association of Law
    Libraries (AALL), 85
American Chemical Society, Paragon
    peer review software of, 126
American Geophysical Union (AGU),
    31,128

American Institute of Physics, 33
American Library Association (ALA),
    85
American Medical Association, 35
Anaesthesia and Intensive Care, 30
Annual reports, preserving and
    disseminating source for
    business history, 107-118
    digitizing-related issues, 115-118
    history of accounting and finance,
        108
    history of graphic design and
        advertising, 108-109,110f
    history of technology, 109,111f
    introduction to, 108-113,110f-112f
    placing reports on Web, 113-114
    processing report, 114-115,115f
    social, political, and economic
        history, 109,112f,113
    unrealized research potential, 113
Annual Reviews, Inc., 37
ARCH-way project, 11
ARL. *See* Association of Research
    Libraries (ARL)
arXiv, 72
Association of Research Libraries
    (ARL), 52,57
Association of Subscription Agents, 33

Bacvhrach, 52
BALANCE Act of 2003, 91,93
Balanced Access Model, 130-131
Baltimore & Ohio Rail Road Company,
    108,109,111f,112f
Bear, G., 118

Behavior(s), information-seeking,
    electronic reference works
    for, library budgeting for,
    50-52
Benefit Authors without Limiting
    Advancement or Net
    Consumer Expectations
    (BALANCE) Act of 2003,
    91,93
Bichteler, J., 51
"Big Deal," 16
BioMed Central, 72,129,132
Bishop, W.W., 49
Blackwell Publishers, 30,39
BMJ Journals Library Resource Centre
    (LRC), 38
B&O Rail Road, 108,109,111f,112f
Book(s), electronic, 8-9
Books in Print, 158
British Dental Journal, 30
Brown, C., 53
Brown University, 56
Bruegel, M., 102
Bruno Business Library, at University
    of Alabama, 108
Budgeting, library, electronic reference
    works and, 47-62. *See also*
    Library budgeting, electronic
    reference works and
Business history, preserving and
    disseminating source for,
    annual reports in, 107-118.
    See also Annual reports,
    preserving and disseminating
    source for business history

Canadian Institute for Scientific and
    Technical Information
    (CISTI), 78
Cardiff University, School of Engineering
    at, ejournals at, 63-74
    acquisition procedures, 65
    decision to go e-only, 67
        acquisitions processes in, 67-70
        managing process in, 70-71

funding of, 64-65
future developments in, 71-73
introduction to, 64
NESLI and UK ejournals policy,
    65-66
usage of, 66-67
Caren, L., 51
Carlson, S., 53
CatchWord, 19
CD-ROM, 146
Cell Press, 32
Chambers, M.B., 104
Chemnetbase, 59
Child, W., 49
Cicovacki, P., 104
CISTI. *See* Canadian Institute for
    Scientific and Technical
    Information (CISTI)
Cleary, D.E., 135
Cole, L., 18,31,36
Collection development, impact of
    copyright law on, 83-97
Columbia School of Library Science,
    49
Columbia University, 48
Commissioner of Education, 57
Condron, P., 19
Confederate Army, 109
Congress, 85,91,95
Cooper-Hewitt Museum, 108
Copyright, described, 84-85
Copyright Act of 1976, 93
Copyright challenges, future, for
    libraries, 94-95
Copyright Clearance Center, 130
Copyright law, impact on library
    acquisitions and collection
    development of electronic
    resources, 83-97
    case law, 91-94
    CTEA, 88-89
    current legislation, 91
    DMCA, 86-88
    Eldred v. Ashcroft, 537 US 186 (2003),
        91-93

future copyright challenges for
    libraries, 94-95
introduction to, 84
legislation, 85-91
New York Times Co., Inc. v. Tasini,
    533 US 483 (2001), 93-94
UCITA, 89-91
Copyright Term Extension Act
    (CTEA), 88-89,91-92
Cornell University, 72
Council PRC, 32
COUNTER initiative, 127,139
Counting Online Usage of Networked
    Electronic Resources
    (COUNTER) initiative,
    127,139
Crawshaw, L., 23,36,40
CRC Handbook of Chemistry and
    Physics, 54,59
Cronin-Kardon, C.L., 107
Crothers, S., 15
CTEA. *See* Sonny Bono Copyright
    Term Extension Act (CTEA)

DA Information Inc., 19
DA Information Services, 27
Dangerous Properties of Industrial
    Materials, 59
Database(s)
    Oracle, 114
    subscribing to
        criteria for, 100
        importance of indexing in, 99-106
            general issues in, 104-105
            introduction to, 100
            methodology in, 100-101
            results of, 101-104
    Web of Knowledge, of ISI, 64
de Gruyter, W., 23
"Death and the Maiden," 103
Decryption, 86
DeLong, L., 99

Department of Electronics, in
    institutional challenges to
    increased library provision of
    electronic materials, 11-12
Depression, 114
Der Prozess, 104
"Der Tod und das Madchen," 103
Dialog, 51,94
Differential Pricing Model, 130-131
Digital Content Forum, 70
Digital Millennium Copyright Act
    (DMCA), 86-88,91
Digitizing, of annual reports for
    preserving and disseminating
    source for business history,
    issues related to, 115-118
    accessibility, 118
    color *vs.* black and white, 116-117
    file size, 117-118
    image resolutions, 117
    OCR process, 117
    scanning, 116
Divine/RoweCom debacle, 34
DMCA. *See* Digital Millennium
    Copyright Act (DMCA)
Drexel University, 67
DSPACE repository, 132
Duranceau, E.F., 22

Early English Books Online, 8
EBSCO, 4-5,15,20,80,100,101,103,104
Edwards, L., 49
E-journal(s)
    deconstruction of, incentives for,
        135-144
        comfort tradition bound
            academics, 143
        computer departments, 141-142
        introduction to, 136
        measurable impact of faculty
            publications, 139
        meeting demand, 139-140
        peer review, 137-138
        P&T process, 138-139

systematic access, 140-141
universities taking back
    knowledge, 142
at School of Engineering at Cardiff
    University, 63-74. *See also*
    Cardiff University, School of
    Engineering at, ejournals at
E-journal administrators, role of, 16-17
E-Journal Only project, 11
Eldred v. Ashcroft, 537 US 186 (2003),
    91-93
Electronic books, 8-9
Electronic journal delivery, in
    academic libraries, 15-45.
    See also Academic libraries,
    electronic journal delivery in
Electronic materials
    academics and, 10-11
    increased library provision of,
        institutional challenges to,
        3-14
        Department of Electronics in,
        11-12
    electronic books, 8-9
    electronic short loan, 7
    introduction to, 4
    student perceptions of, 6-7
Electronic reference works, library
    budgeting and, 47-62. *See
    also* Library budgeting,
    electronic reference works
    and
Electronic resources
    impact of copyright law on library
        acquisitions and collection
        development on, 83-97
    print resources *vs.*, 52-53
Electronic serials, in academic
    libraries, 75-82
    introduction to, 75-76
    reference services' role in, 81
Electronic short loan, 7
Elsevier, 28,29,33,79
    ScienceDirect e-journals service, 64
Elsevier journals, 78

Emerald site, 23-24
Encyclopaedia of Life Sciences, 8
ENGIN. *See* School of Engineering
    (ENGIN)
English Poetry Full Text Database, 8
Engnetbase, 54
Enhanced online access
    alternative methods for, 120-121
    infrastructure of, changes in,
        reasons for making, 121
    new systems in, integration of,
        121-123
    redesigned delivery options for,
        119-134
        alternative journal cost model
            options, 129-130
        example alternative journal
            distribution approaches,
            131-132
        example transactional agent
            model, 130-131
        librarians involvement in,
            123-128
        alternative distribution and peer
            review options, 125-126
        described, 123-124
        P&T process, 124-125
        tools for accountability, 127-128
        value for dollars, 126-127
    new paradigm models, 128-134
    online book options, 132-134
    profiles by agents, 134
Ennis, L., 52
*Essays by Lewis White Beck: Five
    Decades as a Philosopher*,
    104

Factiva, 94
Faculty publications, measurable
    impact of, in incentives for
    deconstruction of e-journals,
    139
FEDORA, 122
Flesher, D.L., 108

Frankfurt Group, 70
Funding, library, 56-58
Funk, M., 36

Gale Group, 94
Geleijnse, H., 78
Genetics, 22
Ginsparg, 52
Good, S., 145
Google, 140
Great Depression, 114
'Green Library,' 50
Green, S., 50
Guarneri Quarter, 103
Guyer, P., 101

Halperin, M., 107
Hamaker, C., 28
Harnard, 52
Harvard Board of Governors, 48
Harvard Overseers, 48
HERON, 7
HighWire, 37-38
Hill, C., 20
Historical Corporate Annual Reports
  Collection, at Lippincott
  Library at University of
  Pennsylvania, 107
Holoviak, J.C., 32
Hudson Motor Car Company, 109,110f
Human Molecular Genetics, 27
Humanities Index, 100,101,102,103,
  104
Hutchins, M., 49

IEE, 11
IEEE, 37
IEEE Explore Ejournal package, 11-2
IEEE publications, 69
IEEE transactions, 69
IEEEXplore service, 69

IEL, 37
ILL rights, 140
Indexing, importance in databases,
  99-106. *See also* Database(s),
  subscribing to, importance of
  indexing in
Information Alchemist, at Manhattan
  College Library, 21
Information Resource and Access
  Policy (IRAP), 11
Information Services division
  (INFOS), 64,66,70-71,73
Information-seeking behavior,
  electronic reference works
  for, library budgeting for,
  50-52
INFOS. *See* Information Services
  division (INFOS)
Ingenta, 20,23,38
Ingenta Select, 19,20,23
Institute of Electrical and Electronics
  Engineers, Inc., 69
Institutional challenges, to increased
  library provision of electronic
  materials, 3-14. *See also*
  Electronic materials,
  increased library provision
  of, institutional challenges to
Interlibrary Loan (ILL) rights, 140
International Journal of Epidemiology,
  27
Internet, 52
Internet2, 60
Iowa State University, 51
IRAP (Information Resource and
  Access Policy), 11
ISI, Web of Knowledge databases of,
  64

Jasper, R., 28
J.B. Morrell University Library, 5,9
JISC. *See* Joint Information Systems
  Committee (JISC)
Johnson, G.J., 3

Johnston, B.J., 56
Joint Information Systems Committee
    (JISC), 66,72

Kafka, 104
Kalyan, S., 80
Kant and the Claims of Taste, 101
Kant, I., 99,101
Katz, B., 2
Khanna, D., 118
King, P., 23
King, R., 118
*Kirk Othmer's Encyclopedia of
    Chemical Technology*, 54
Kluwer, 79
Knovel, 59
Kremer, J.M., 54
Kritik der Urteilskraft, 101
Kroeger, A., 49
Kyrillidou, M., 57,60

Lange's Handbook of Chemistry, 54
Lawal, I.O., 47,52
Leddy Library, of University of
    Windsor, Canada, 75-82
Lee, L.A., 83
"Lewis White Beck on Reasons and
    Causes," 104
Lexis, 93-94
Lexis-Nexis, 51
Leyden, 56
Leysen, J.M., 52
Li, S., 2
Librarian(s)
    involvement in enhanced online
        access, 123-128. *See also*
        Enhanced online access,
        redesigned delivery options
        for, librarians involvement in
    practical and policy issues for,
        145-160. *See also* PDA
        serials
    innovations–presence or absence
        of, 146-147

Librarians' Conference of 1853, 50
Librarianship, as conversation,
    159-160
Libraries of Oxford and Cambridge, 48
Library(ies)
    academic
        electronic journal delivery in,
            15-45. *See also* Academic
            libraries, electronic journal
            delivery in
        electronic serials in, 75-82
        print serials in, 76-77
    future copyright challenges for,
        94-95
    provision of electron materials by,
        institutional challenges to,
        3-14. *See also* Electronic
        materials, increased library
        provision of, institutional
        challenges to
Library acquisitions, impact of
    copyright law on, 83-97
Library budgeting, electronic reference
    works and, 47-62
    described, 58-59
    information-seeking behavior,
        50-52
    introduction to, 48
    library funding, 56-58
    origin of reference work, 49-50
    print *vs.* electronic, 52-53
Library funding, 56-58
Library Journal, 136
Lippincott Electronic Delivery Service,
    114
Lippincott, J., III, 114
Lippincott Library, 114,118
    at University of Pennsylvania,
        Historical Corporate Annual
        Reports Collection, 107,118
LIS-E-Journals, 31
LRC. *See* BMJ Journals Library
    Resource Centre (LRC)
Lynden, F.C., 56,58

Manhattan College Library,
    Information Alchemist at, 21
MARC records, 71,141
MD Consult, 54
Menefee, D., 28
MetaPress, 25,26
Micromedia ProQuest, 100
Model Site License, 66
Morse, C., 23

National Electronic Site License
    Initiative (NESLI) policy,
    65-66,68
National E-University, 9
Nature, use of science reference texts
    and, 53-56,55t
Neal, 52
NESLI (National Electronic Site
    License Initiative) policy,
    65-66,68
netLibrary, 8
New York Times Co., Inc. v. Tasini,
    533 US 483 (2001), 93-94
Next Generation Initiative (NGI), 60
NGI. *See* Next Generation Initiative
    (NGI)
1963 Eastman-Kodak report, 108
Norman, F., 34

OCR processing. *See* Optical character
    recognition (OCR)
    processing
Office of Fair Trading, of UK, 71
Online access, enhanced, redesigned
    delivery options for, 119-134.
    See also Enhanced online
    access, redesigned delivery
    options for
Online journals, access to, activation
    of, 17-22
Open Access Metadata Harvesters, 72
OpenURL 2.0, 122

Optical character recognition (OCR)
    processing, 114,115,117
Oracle database, 114
Orr, C., 33
Oster, D., 24
Oxford University, 7

Paint Shop Pro, 114,116
Paragon peer review software, of
    American Chemical Society,
    126
PDA serials, 145-160
    acquisition of
        hidden costs of, 154-156
        as option for libraries, 148-149
        reasons for, 156-159
    allureness of, 150-151
    free, library and, 151-153
    hybrid nature of, 147-148
    indicative of blurring of distinctions
        within library acquisitions,
        153-154
    innovations–presence or absence of,
        146-147
    introduction to, 146
    left to patrons on their own, 149
    as medium rather than format, 150
Pelzer, N.L., 51,52
Penn Library Systems, 114
Penn Library Systems Department,
    114
Periodicals Research II (Micromedia
    ProQuest), 100,101,102,103
Perry's Chemical Engineers
    Handbook, 54
Personal digital assistant (PDA),
    hybrid nature of, 147-148
Personal digital assistant (PDA)
    serials, 145-160. *See also*
    PDA serials
Photoshop, 114,116
Picerno, P., 28
Pinfield, S., 29

Piracy Deterrence and Education Act
    of 2003, 91
PloS Biology, 72
Pober, S., 21
Porter, G., 37
Prabhu, M., 15
Previts, G.J., 108
Price Waterhouse Company, 113-114
Pricing issues, electronic journal
        delivery in academic libraries
        and, 29-33
Print resources, electronic resources
        vs., 52-53
Print serials, in academic libraries,
        76-77
Project Muse, 105
Promotion and tenure (P&T) process,
        138-139
    in enhanced online access, 124-125
Properties of Organic Compounds, 59
ProQuest, 79,94
P&T process. *See* Promotion and
        tenure (P&T) process
Public Domain Enhancement Act, 91
Public Library of Science, 72
Public Service Librarianship, 140
Publishers, for online subscriptions,
        24-29
PubMed Central, 72
PubsCom, 32

RALPHY electronic reserve project,
        7,11
Reference and Information funds, 65
Reference and Information group, 65
Reference services, in electronic serials
        in academic libraries, 81
Reference texts, science, use of, nature
        and, 53-56,55t
Reference works
    electronic, library budgeting and,
        47-62. *See also* Library
        budgeting, electronic
        reference works and
    origin of, 49-50

*Report on Public Libraries in the
        United States* of 1876, 50
Rowley, J., 105
Royal Society of Chemistry, 30
Rupp-Serrano, K., 78

Samson, W.D., 108
Sax, 59
SCETI. *See* Schoenberg Center for
        Electronic Text & Image
        (SCETI)
Schoenberg Center for Electronic Text
        & Image (SCETI), 114
Scholarly Publications and Academic
        Resources Coalition
        (SPARC), 72
School of Engineering (ENGIN),
        67-70
School of Engineering, at Cardiff
        University, ejournals at,
        63-74. *See also* Cardiff
        University, School of
        Engineering at, ejournals at
Schubert, F., 103-104
Science, Technology and Medicine
        (STM), 47
Science reference texts, use of, nature
        and, 53-56,55t
ScienceDirect, 69
ScienceDirect ejournals service, of
        Elsevier, 64
Serial(s)
    electronic, in academic libraries,
        75-82. *See also* Electronic
        serials, in academic libraries
    print, in academic libraries, 76-77
SerialsSolutions electronic journals
        management system, 71
Sinha, R., 35
*Sittigs Handbook of Toxic and
        Hazardous Chemicals and
        Carcinogens* (4th ed.), 59
Slack, E., 118
Society for General Microbiology, 34

Somerville, A., 51
Sonny Bono Copyright Term
    Extension Act (CTEA), 88
Southern Universities Purchasing
    Consortium (SUPC), 65
SPARC (Scholarly Publications and
    Academic Resources
    Coalition), 72
SPARC Alternatives, 72
Sprague, N., 104
Springer LINK, 39,40
Springer Verlag, 40
Standards, 56,58
Steinhardt, A., 103
Stern, D., 119
Stevens, Justice, 92
STM. *See* Science, Technology and
    Medicine (STM)
Stone, G., 23
Su, D., 2
Sullivan, S., 15
SUPC. *See* Southern Universities
    Purchasing Consortium
    (SUPC)
Swets Blackwell Inc., 19,20,22,29,65,
    68

Taylor & Francis, 25
Tenopir, C., 52,81
The City University of New York
    PSC–CUNY Research Award
    Program, 2
The Gentleman's Magazine, 4
*The Journal of Aesthetics and Art
    Criticism*, 101
The New York Times, 94
Trial, 104
Turner, R., 17,18,27
2001 Research Assessment Exercise, 64

UCITA. *See* Uniform Computer
    Information Transactions Act
    (UCITA)

UK ejournals policy, 65-66
UK E–University Project, 9
*Ullmans Encyclopedia of Industrial
    Chemistry*, 54
Uniform Commercial Code, 90
Uniform Computer Information
    Transactions Act (UCITA),
    89-91
United States Code, 85,86,94
University of Alabama, Bruno
    Business Library at, 108
University of Hertfordshire, 23
University of Idaho, 53
University of Illinois–Chicago, 53
University of Leeds, 18
University of Melbourne,
    16,18,19,21,25,27,41
University of Melbourne LINK, 39-40
University of North
    Carolina–Charlotte, 28
University of Oklahoma, 53
University of Pennsylvania, Lippincott
    Library at, Historical
    Corporate Annual Reports
    Collection, 107
University of Wales College of
    Medicine, 64-65
University of Windsor, Canada, Leddy
    Library of, 75-82
University of York, 3
University of York Library, 4

Value Added Tax (VAT), 69-70
Veterinary Bulletin, 51
Virtual library environments (VLEs),
    3,9
Virtual Private Networking (VPN)
    access, 141
VLEs. *See* Virtual library
    environments (VLEs)
Voigt, M.J., 53
von Foerster, T., 33
Voyager catalogue, 71

Voyager library management system,
    65
Voyager OPAC, 66
VPN access. *See* Virtual Private
    Networking (VPN) access

Wallenius, L.I.T., 75
Ward, D., 51
Web of Knowledge databases, of ISI,
    64
WebCT system, 9
Westlaw, 93-94
Wharton School, 108,114
White Rose Consortium of
    Universities Grid project, 9

Wicks, R., 101
Wiese, W.H., 52
Wiley InterScience, 39,79,128
Wilson, 79
Wilson Omnifile, 80
Wolf, M., 63
World War II, 114
World Wide Web, 51
Wu, M.M., 83

Yale College Library, 48
Yale Trustees, 48
Yamaguchi, M., 18

BOOK ORDER FORM!

Order a copy of this book with this form or online at:
http://www.HaworthPress.com/store/product.asp?sku= 5729

Collection Development Issues
in the Online Environment

—— in softbound at $19.95 ISBN-13: 978-0-7890-3087-0 / ISBN-10: 0-7890-3087-X.
—— in hardbound at $34.95 ISBN-13: 978-0-7890-3086-3 / ISBN-10: 0-7890-3086-1.

COST OF BOOKS _____

POSTAGE & HANDLING _____
US: $4.00 for first book & $1.50
for each additional book
Outside US: $5.00 for first book
& $2.00 for each additional book.

SUBTOTAL _____

In Canada: add 7% GST. _____

STATE TAX _____
CA, IL, IN, MN, NJ, NY, OH, PA & SD residents
please add appropriate local sales tax.

FINAL TOTAL _____
If paying in Canadian funds, convert
using the current exchange rate,
UNESCO coupons welcome.

❏ BILL ME LATER:
Bill-me option is good on US/Canada/
Mexico orders only; not good to jobbers,
wholesalers, or subscription agencies.

❏ Signature _____

❏ Payment Enclosed: $_____

❏ PLEASE CHARGE TO MY CREDIT CARD:

❏ Visa ❏ MasterCard ❏ AmEx ❏ Discover
❏ Diner's Club ❏ Eurocard ❏ JCB

Account #_____

Exp Date_____

Signature_____
(Prices in US dollars and subject to change without notice.)

PLEASE PRINT ALL INFORMATION OR ATTACH YOUR BUSINESS CARD

Name

Address

City   State/Province   Zip/Postal Code

Country

Tel   Fax

May we use your e-mail address for confirmations and other types of information? ❏Yes ❏No We appreciate receiving
your e-mail address. Haworth would like to e-mail special discount offers to you, as a preferred customer.
We will never share, rent, or exchange your e-mail address. We regard such actions as an invasion of your privacy.

Order from your **local bookstore** or directly from
The Haworth Press, Inc. 10 Alice Street, Binghamton, New York 13904-1580 • USA
Call our toll-free number (1-800-429-6784) / Outside US/Canada: (607) 722-5857
Fax: 1-800-895-0582 / Outside US/Canada: (607) 771-0012
E-mail your order to us: orders@HaworthPress.com

For orders outside US and Canada, you may wish to order through your local
sales representative, distributor, or bookseller.
For information, see http://HaworthPress.com/distributors

(Discounts are available for individual orders in US and Canada only, not booksellers/distributors.)

Please photocopy this form for your personal use.
www.HaworthPress.com

BOF06